The First Comers

AGAIN: *for* ERIC DOUGLAS

THE FIRST

COMERS

Indians of America's Dawn

by Alice Marriott

Illustrated by Harvey Weiss

David McKay Company, Inc.
New York

THE FIRST COMERS

COPYRIGHT © 1960

BY ALICE MARRIOTT

PUBLISHED SIMULTANEOUSLY IN THE DOMINION OF CANADA

FIRST EDITION AUGUST 1960
REPRINTED JULY 1962
JUNE   1966
NOVEMBER 1968

LIBRARY OF CONGRESS CATALOG CARD NUMBER 60–9878

Printed in the United States of America

Contents

Foreword

FOREWORDS PROBABLY SHOULD BE CALLED HINDWORDS. THEY are written last; it might be better if they were read at the end of the book, instead of at its beginning. The rules of the publishing game, however, establish that the foreword should come first, so here, for those who will read it, it is.

This is not a book for archaeologists. It is not a history of the American Indians. It is not a textbook in anthropology. It is not a do-it-yourself book about digging up the past.

This book is intended to be a guidebook. I would like other people to feel some of the excitement I have felt—say, at the moment I saw my first man-made mound rising up from a corn-field and knew in an instant, without being told—just knew —that it had been raised by men and women, not by the forces of nature. I would like other people to know the care that controls my hands, and that keeps them from shaking with that same excitement, when, in the museum laboratory, I begin to reconstruct a shattered bowl, my palms following the same curves that the woman who built it modeled a hundred and a hundred years ago.

Most especially I should like to give to other people the sense of sharing and belonging that is a part of archaeology in the field and in the museum. Tennyson made Ulysses say, "I am a part of all that I have met." It is a good motto for anybody; it is a necessary motto for those of us who are interested in the peoples of the past.

History—and, beyond it, archaeology—is not dates and battles, or the maneuverings of politicians. History and archaeology are the lives of human beings: of men, women, and children, who felt and acted and believed much as we do, even though their material surroundings and circumstances were not like ours in many ways.

I have read many pages of knowledgeable writings in preparing this book, and a list of publications will be found in the back of it. The list is not included to prove to anybody that I have tried to find out what I am talking about. The list is there to give you—the reader—a springboard from which you may plunge into the world of digs and museums, laboratories and libraries, that is, the world of archaeologists. The bibliography has been divided by subject, so that you can look up the part of a very large field of study that interests you most, and can find out more about it than is set down here.

So many people have helped through the work of so many years that I cannot even try to list their names. It would be worse to forget even one than not to mention any. To all of you, wherever you are, whether you know that I am thinking about you or not, my thanks.

Alice Marriott

Oklahoma City, Oklahoma
January 9, 1960

The First Comers

1 It's a Long Word

JUST SUPPOSE THAT YOU WOKE UP ONE MORNING AND FOUND THAT the past was gone. Imagine what your world would be like if there were nothing left in it but the things that have been invented or discovered since 1900.

There would be no wheels to turn, and no steam or gasoline engines to turn them. There would be no electric lights to turn on when night came. There would be no sidewalks and no asphalt pavements, and there would be no automobiles or buses to travel them. No airplanes would cross the sky; there would be only trees and clouds above you. You would be naked, because no clothing would be left for you to wear.

You could neither read nor write, for paper, ink, and the alphabet would all have disappeared. You could not count, for the numbers to count with would not exist. You could not even speak to other people, nor understand them if they spoke to you, for you would all lack words, although you would have kept the power of speech.

If you held two fruits in your hands, each red and shiny, you could tell them apart only because one was hard and the other was soft. You would have no way of knowing that one was called an apple and the other a tomato; that they were first cultivated in different hemispheres; or whether the first people to grow them looked alike or had similar customs.

The world's past is a part of all of us; so much a part of each of us that we do not even know that it is there. Everything that we do and have today has its roots somewhere in the past of mankind. We take this fact for granted; indeed, we take it so much for granted that we have had to invent a special word to designate the people who study the far past, just as we have invented a word for the study of the times that are gone.

The past that has been written down as it happened, and that can be read, is called history. The men and women who study the written records of the past are called historians. They work from letters and diaries and old account books; from newspapers and magazines long out of date, and from the books that earlier historians have written. These are their tools for learning what happened to the people who walked the earth before them.

But back beyond history in the story of humanity there is a time when writing had not been invented. We know it as the age of prehistory. Usually the study of prehistory is called archaeology, a name that is derived from two Greeks words, "archaeos"—of the past—and "logia"—discourse. Students of archaeology are called archaeologists. They cannot work with the written tools of the historians, for when history begins archaeology ends. Instead, archaeologists study the artifacts made by prehistoric peoples: their tools, whatever is left of their clothing, their cooking utensils, their works of art, the objects they used in worship, their weapons, their games and toys, and sometimes their bones or the bones of their domestic animals; the game animals and birds they hunted, and the pets they kept. Such things were either lost or abandoned by accident when prehistoric peoples moved from place to place, or they were intentionally buried as offerings to the dead with their bodies.

Prehistory can have happened thousands of years ago. It can have happened within the last two hundred years. How old or new prehistory may be depends on what peoples and places we happen to be talking about. Sometimes prehistoric artifacts are easy to find and date. Sometimes archaeologists search for years, trying to locate cities that once stood proudly and then fell into ruins long before our own ancestors were born. In some areas you can find prehistoric artifacts by walking down the right street; in others you must dive to the bottom of the ocean or of a deep lake to discover them.

Often archaeologists begin their study of the past with a written record, and then work backward from it to find the place that was written about. The sites of Troy and of Ur of the Chaldees were discovered in this way by archaeologists working in Asia Minor. So were many of the prehistoric Indian settlements along our own rivers. More and more, as time goes on, the archaeologists are learning to ask for the help of the historians. They also ask for the help of geologists, botanists, biologists, physicists, and medical doctors and technicians. As you read this book, you will begin to see what other sciences have contributed to archaeology.

Some people say that finding artifacts—artifacts are any objects that have been made by men, from stone hammers to jet planes—is like living a detective story. The people who went before us have left us clues to help unravel the mystery of the past. We must track down the clues in order to know what the story is about and how it ended.

Others say that fitting the artifacts into their proper places in human lives is like working a jigsaw puzzle. Before we can recognize the picture, we must find all the pieces and fit them into their proper places. Whatever you want to call it, the business of solving the problem of how human beings have lived —whether or not they resembled us physically, what they knew, what they had, what they believed—is one of the biggest and most exciting games in the world for its players.

It is a game that never grows old, a game that never ends. Just as soon as archaeologists begin to think that they have solved all the problems of one small piece of prehistory and can sit down to take a well-earned rest, a new bone is found, or two pieces of pottery discovered in two different sites are proved to have been made at the same time and place, and the game starts all over again. The new round—once it has begun

—must go on until the new series of questions has been answered, and by the time those solutions are neatly polished off and in place, it will be time to begin the next round with some new discoveries.

The best thing about this endless game is that everyone can win—*if the players follow the rules.* If the rules are broken, everyone loses. Whatever new facts anyone learns can become yours, for all the knowledge of the past can belong to each of us who wants a share of it. It is already part of us, and when we know how large a part of our lives comes from the past, we are richer than before in understanding. Understanding other people, and, through that, understanding ourselves. As long as there are archaeologists to guide us, we cannot help learning and interpreting more and more about ourselves and our neighbors everywhere in the world. As time goes on, we cannot avoid seeing more and more clearly that people are more alike than they are different from one another.

When an archaeologist begins to describe a people of the past, he sets out to reconstruct a world he has never seen, and never will see. With only the smallest surviving fragments, plus his own intelligence and knowledge, he tries to bring to life again a way of living. Languages, religions, sayings, songs, dances, and music will be lacking from his reconstructed world; at best the archaeologist can only make informed guesses about such intangible things.

Clothing and shoe leather, wooden implements, baskets and

blankets and bodies often rot away when they are buried. Only their impressions are left in the earth that has enveloped them. Still, even from these natural casts, a great deal about the objects, their users, and their makers, can be learned by anyone who will give time and patience to studying them. Each fact that is learned from an object may be made to apply to other peoples, other objects.

You can play the archaeology game better, and enjoy it more, if you know something about it to begin with. A skillful player has a better time than a clumsy one, whatever game he happens to be playing. Luckily, it is not hard to learn the basic ground rules of archaeology. There is a great deal of space and time to cover in playing it. There are many objects to be observed and placed in their proper relations to one another. At first the game and the vast field it covers may seem bewildering and puzzling.

And it is quite true that no one person will ever learn all there is to know about the men and women and children of the past. But all the same, anyone who wants to can learn how to find out about the prehistoric people he is particularly interested in. When you know how to *look*—how to look things up in books or examine them in museum cases—then you know *how* to play the archaeology game. Once you have learned the theory of the game, it is up to you to decide whether or not you want to go on playing it. You can decide whether to increase your skill or give up the whole idea. Still, what have you to lose by learning how the experts play the game?

Because we all live on one continent—North America—let us concentrate, in this basic rule book, on the archaeology that is nearest to us in space and time. Let's think and talk only about the archaeology of North America. Let's begin with what is known of its original inhabitants—with the people who lived here before the white men came to introduce the writing of history from western Europe. Let's confine ourselves to the American Indians.

2 Who, What, When, Where, and How?

IT IS A RULE OF NEWSPAPER AND MAGAZINE WRITING THAT ANY good news item, or story of any kind, begins with the answers to these questions: *Who did what, when, where, and how?* And, if you can find it out, Why?

In archaeology, we are concerned with getting answers to those same questions. Not only do we start with the questions, though, we often end with them—and with no positive answers. All the same, who, what, when, where, and how remain the signposts of the jumping-off place.

To begin with the who, who were the Americans of the past, and what did they look like? Can we describe them? Were they, and are their descendants, related to any other groups of human beings in the world? After all, we are more concerned with people and the lives they lived than with anything else. In order to leave traces of their lives behind them, people must have lived and worked, thought, felt, and hoped. Who were these people?

All human beings, wherever they live, are divided into three main groups, on the basis of physical structure. We call these groups the *races of mankind.* "Race," as archaeologists use the word, means only the *physical* subdivisions of humanity. Race has nothing to do with language, religion, technical skill, cooking, washing, or manufactures. "Race" in this sense means solely what people *look* like—what traits can be handed down from parents to children.

Naturally, since there have been human beings on the earth for a long time, since they have wandered from continent to continent, and have married members of other races for centuries, there are no *pure* races left. The best we can hope for is to find a few individuals in each race who combine the physical characteristics that are typical of other members of the same race stock. Even then, these people who can be described as representative of the purest forms of their racial stocks may have children who do not look like them, who may even resemble members of other races. That is because everyone who lives carries within himself the minute *genes* he has inherited from his long succession of ancestors. Sometimes one *genetic strain* is *dominant* in an individual, but *recessive,* or hidden, in his children.

So remember that the next few paragraphs will apply only to general population groups, and not to every individual in each group. If you have a thousand individuals from each race to study at one time, you will find that what is said here applies to the average of the group. If you have only one person to study at a time, some of these standards will apply, but all of them certainly won't. Knowledge gathered from the study of groups should always be applied to the further study of other groups, not to their individual members.

In general, then, the race whose members have dark skins; dark, curly hair; dark eyes; full, out-turned lips; blunt, flat noses; and legs and arms that are long in proportion to the length of their bodies, is called the *Negroid* race.

The race whose members have yellow-toned skins; dark, straight hair; eyelids folded at the corners so that the eyes appear to slant upward and outward; medium-full lips and medium-sharp noses; with arms and legs that are short in proportion to body length, is called the *Mongoloid* race.

The race that has a reddish skin tone; light to dark and straight to curly hair; light to dark eyes; rather narrow lips and rather sharp noses; with a medium-length proportion between limbs and body, is called the *Caucasoid* race.

Each of the great race stocks has many subdivisions. We are not going into any of them in detail here and now. Thick books, and many of them, have been written on this special subject. The study of physical anthropology, as we call the science of races in America, is a wide field in itself. We are interested in it now only for its contributions to our own interest: archaeology.

There are more living members, all around the world, of the

Mongoloid race than there are of either of the other two great stocks. The Negroid race is the next largest. The smallest of all is the Caucasoid, but, because most modern North Americans are Caucasoids and we are used to looking at one another, we often assume that we are more numerous than we really are. We are likely to forget that we are a racial minority in the world at large.

The American Indians, who, as we have already said, are the subject of this book, form a subgroup of the Mongoloid race. This is clear when you compare pictures of Indians with pictures of Chinese, Japanese, Koreans, or Tibetans. Today, most of the Mongoloids live in Asia and the islands adjoining that continent. Probably the ancestors of the modern American Indians were Asians. They left their homes about the end of the last ice age and moved eastward.

When we think of peoples' migrating from one continent to another, we think of thousands of human beings moving, all at one time, all from one place to another. We think of them as making the same plans and preparations, and setting out for their new homes, all at once and all together. Playing the archaeology game would be easier for everybody if that had happened. It didn't.

One of the safety islands for thinking things over in the archaeology game, like a "rest" in hopscotch or parcheesi, is a phrase that all scientists, including archaeologists and historians, use over and over again. It is a useful phrase, good to know and handy to have around, whatever you are doing. It is *as far as we know now*. Keep it in mind, because it is going to be repeated again and again throughout this book. The repetition is essential because next week—after I finish writing or you finish reading—some archaeologist may make a whole new set of discoveries. Possibly they will contradict everything that is said here. All the same, what is said now is believed to be true.

So, as far as we know now, the ancestral Indians came from several different regions in Asia. They probably left their homes for many different reasons. Perhaps—almost certainly—they spoke many different languages, although we do not know what those languages were. Above all, the first migrants did not travel all together—or even in the same century or millennium. They must have journeyed in very small groups—a few friends, relatives, or families, at a time. They traveled slowly, and each journey lasted through a long period of years.

During the years of their traveling, ice sheets advanced across North America from the Arctic Circle to southern Kansas, and retreated again to the north that we know now. Of course the ice sheets were not unbroken, or even solidly continuous. Corridors were left, along the mountain ranges and the valleys of great rivers, except for the few years when the glaciation reached its peak. People and animals could continue to exist and to move around in restricted areas. That is probably why artifacts are found in some places and not in others, particularly the artifacts belonging to the earliest times of migration. Probably, too, some people came east for short periods of time, and then returned to Asia, while others went back and forth at will and at random.

Thus the earth's surface changed around the migrants as they moved forward or returned. Water sometimes rose behind

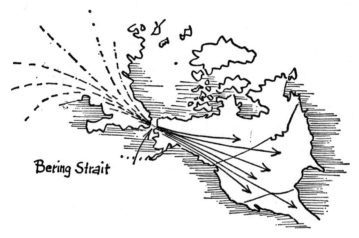

A land bridge once spanned the Bering Strait

them and covered the land where once they walked. Many people were cut off from the homes of their ancestors and of their living relatives. They had little choice left but to go forward to the east, into the New World, and become ancestors themselves.

We believe now that many of the first American Mongoloids crossed a land bridge that once spanned the Bering Strait, connecting Siberia and Alaska. Then the Pacific Ocean remade its bed, and most of the land bridge sank into the sea. Only the peaks of its mountains were left above the surface of the water, to become what we know now as the Diomedes Islands. Geologists tell us that most of these changes took place soon after the end of the last ice age, probably about twenty thousand years ago. It is too soon to tell yet whether the changes have ended. Climatologists and geologists today seem to think that we are living now in an interglacial period, which will end when the earth tips on its axis, changing the water level along our coast lines and bringing ice down across our country. If you think of the age of the earth, and the succession of cold and warm periods it has already gone through, this prediction seems likely to come true.

Let's get back to the first Asiatic immigrants to North America. From the region of Alaska that borders the Bering Strait, they first traveled eastward and inland. They spread out along the coast, too, and began steadily to work their way southward. From the coast, they followed the main river beds upstream, and found that many of the rivers flowed between mountain ranges. So the people, living for a while here, moving on a little farther there, journeyed slowly through the mainlands. They had no reason to hurry. They didn't know exactly where they were going or what they would do when they got there. They had no idea whether they might meet other people—who could be enemies—or dangerous wild animals. Without planning it, the people just kept on moving, following the slopes of the country and seeking the warm weather, finding whatever there was to be found for their food.

As they journeyed across the land, the old groups separated and new ones were formed. Some families or clans stopped in one place, some in another, and some who stopped settled down to stay right where they were. As the original units began to spread out, and the distances among groups widened, each gathering of people began to speak more and more in its own way. Some spoke quite differently from others to begin with, but even groups which had been able to understand each other in the beginning gradually became more and more separated in speech. Some continued to speak with only slight differences, so that when descendants of the original groups met one another later on, they could understand what their new acquaintances were saying. But often time and isolation increased differences in speech that were there in the beginning, and eventually a time came when it was hard to tell whether certain Indian languages were related to one another or not.

What can archaeologists learn about these earliest peoples? Can they find out anything at all? Or can they only guess, and pass the guesses along to the rest of us for what they are worth?

One good way to begin studying the first migrants is to make lists of the things different tribes of American Indians have in common besides their race. If we can discover customs or artifacts that are about the same in every known tribe of

American Indians, then the chances are that those habits or objects are old in origin. Quite possibly, when something is widely distributed, it will be something that the first adventurers knew about and brought with them when they set out from Asia.

Early emigrants from Asia knew how to make fire by friction

It seems as if they all knew how to make fire by friction, that is, by rubbing a soft piece of wood with a harder one until the soft one is heated and begins to smoke and smolder. The oldest human remains in Asia show that the earliest men had some knowledge of fire.

All American Indians seem to have some knowledge of working in stone to make tools and weapons. Because of the kind of stonework they produced, we think they must have been men of the late Paleolithic or Old Stone Age. In the dawn of time, men used whatever stones they found that were naturally shaped to a convenient size and form. They may have shaped their implements slightly by chipping one stone against another, but that was as far as they went. In the Paleolithic—the Old Stone Age—craftsmen discovered that by hammering and, later, by pressing down—on certain kinds of stones with pieces of wood or bone or antler, they could peel off chips of the stone, and so make knife blades and points for their weapons. All stones are not suitable for this kind of toolmaking. Only certain ones, such as flint, chert, chalcedony, quartz, and some of the semiprecious crystals, can be worked in this way. Granite and tufa will break into chunks that can be ground down, but these stones won't peel. Some kinds of limestone shatter under pressure. Slate and shale, which are made up of thin layers, usually crumble, and sandstone will fall to pieces every time. The early stoneworkers were observant enough to notice and remember the differences among stones, and to find and use the right ones for the purposes they had in mind. They were good, practical geologists.

The earliest Indians must have had dogs. At first, perhaps, they kept dogs for hunting—to find and chase game, and then to attack or hold it until the men could kill it with clubs or spears. Probably some of the largest dogs, even in the earliest days, were used as beasts of burden. They may have been led along, with bundles loaded and tied to their backs, to help their owners move from place to place. And most likely, when there were times of starvation, dogs would be cooked and eaten—as we eat oxen today—because the people could not find any other food. The first Indians may also have wrapped themselves in dogskins when the weather was cold if they had no other animal hides. Dogs were the first animals domesticated, and we have no evidence that the Indians knew of any other domestic animals. So far, no bones of horses, camels, sheep, cattle, pigs, chickens, or other domesticated animals except dogs have been recovered from early Indian sites. They were unknown in North America until the Spaniards introduced them in the 1500's.

We know that when the first Americans went somewhere overland—to a new continent, or along a fishing stream, or over a mountain range and into the next valley, or across a camp to visit their friends—they walked. If they traveled by water, the Indians paddled rafts or canoes. Wheels and sails were invented in Eurasia in the Neolithic Age, but the ancestral Indians seem to have left home without knowing about them, as far as we know now. There is nothing known to show us that Indians knew about wheels until after Europeans "discovered" America.

Let's stop for a moment, and think seriously about what that last sentence means. It means that the lives men lived in the American hemisphere became so different from those of men of the Euroasiatic hemisphere, that we keep on calling the Americas the "New World" to this good day. Actually, of course, the way of life in this world was older than that of the continent from which Columbus sailed. The invention of the wheel had changed everything in the Eastern Hemisphere.

After the wheel was invented, chariots and wagons could roll; clockworks could turn; printing presses could operate; water wheels could be used for irrigation and drainage; steam engines could be employed to supply power for all the wheels—in fact, so many of the things we know and use today depend on the operation of wheels that we are often said to be living in the Age of the Wheel.

The invention of the wheel, followed by the inventions of all the other things that depend on wheels, made a difference in the way men lived but not a difference in the way men thought. The Indians were just as intelligent by nature as were the Europeans. Men's minds worked in the same ways in the Old and New Worlds, but the men were interested in different matters. Instead of concentrating on mechanical engineering, the Indians concentrated on sculpture, and on religious poetry and drama. Instead of domesticating large animals that could draw wagons or carry burdens, and make their owners' lives easier physically, the Indians domesticated turkeys and used their feathers in religious ceremonies. Instead of spinning with wheels or disks, the Indians spun by twisting fibers between the palm of the hand and the thigh. But, like all the men of the

Old World, all the men of the New made poems and plays and songs and stories for themselves and their children; they worshipped; they made musical instruments to accompany their singing, and they danced. Like all men everywhere, they lived.

Even the earliest Indians cooked their food over their friction-made fires, instead of gnawing hunks of raw meat off bones. We know they did this, for we find the cooked bones of game animals in the ashes at the earliest Indian camp sites. The Indians invented a sort of fireless cooker; they heated stones in their fires, and dropped the hot stones into skin-lined holes in the ground, or into bags or baskets of plant fibers that had previously been filled with the ingredients of stew or mush. And in choosing their cooking stones the Indians proved again that they were practical geologists. They were able to distinguish the stones that would heat without splintering or cracking from the ones that would shatter and send a barrage of fragments through the camp when they got hot. The Indians often carried unworked stones—what are called "blanks"—of different kinds around with them, when they moved from one camp to another, to use when they were needed.

These earliest of all Indians must have had an idea that there is a world beyond this one—a life of the spirit that continues when the body dies. They buried their dead reverently, and with the bodies they laid away the possessions people had treasured during their lifetimes: the man's weapons; the woman's cooking stones; the dolls and toys, molded of mud, that a child had played with. The Indians must have wanted the souls of the dead, in their new homes, to find again the work and pleasure they had known upon earth.

There. That is the first round of the archaeology game. We have played it in the public library, with books from the shelves and a piece of paper and a pencil. All we needed to do was look in the books and find out what most Indians had in common. Then we made a list of artifacts and the customs they suggested—what is called a *trait list*—that are found wherever men have lived in the New World.

3 In the High and Far-Off Times

THE NEXT ROUND OF THE ARCHAEOLOGY GAME SHOULD BE PLAYED in a museum. I don't care where you live, if you really look around you, you'll find that there is a museum not too far away for you to visit. (The telephone book is a good place to start looking.) Some museums are larger than others; some have more artifacts in their collections; some have one class of artifact and some have another, but most museums contain samples of the kinds of materials we are going to talk about now.

Before we begin to describe museums and their displays, though, it might be a good idea for us to consider briefly how a museum is *supposed* to be used. Many people seem to have an idea that if they walk into a museum, walk through it, look at the case displays as they pass them, and walk out again, they have *seen* the museum. They are mistaken.

A museum is a book, and when you open its front door you are opening the book and beginning to read its story. Museums are usually divided into sections. There may be a section about rocks and minerals; a section of fossils; a section of stuffed animals—these are often displayed against a series of painted or photomural backgrounds that will suggest the native habitats of the living animals; a section of pioneer life, or historical material of some other period; a section showing articles made and used by living peoples in different parts of the world; and a section of archaeology. Each such area is a chapter of the museum book.

Now if you have gone into the museum with the intention of studying one particular subject, you probably will ask where its displays are, go to that section of the museum and spend most of your time there. If you have come to the museum to look around, without deciding to concentrate on any particular display, sooner or later you will find something that interests you more than the other displays. Without intending to do so, and maybe without even realizing that you are doing it, you will stop before the case that holds that particular display. You will unconsciously spend more time in studying it than you do in looking at all the rest of the collection.

Nowadays, most museum directors are dissatisfied if all they do is show you *things*. The idea is to show you also how the things were used, and what they were used for. If a museum director wants to display a stone knife, for example, he may make a model or a drawing of a hand holding the knife, so you can see at once which end of the blade was the point and which end was once hafted into a handle or grasped in a fist. He may set the knife into the case at about the same height and angle at which it was originally held. He probably will put in case lights that will strike the display in such a way as to show the artifact as its maker saw it. The museum director takes much time, care, thought, and effort to help you see and understand that knife, and through it the man who made and used it. If the director has done his work well, you probably aren't aware that there has been any work done at all. The display looks *right* to you—that is, within a few minutes you see and understand as much as anyone else can or does about the

We can study stone implements in the museum book

knife. You don't have to try to figure out how or if your mind received a message of understanding. Looking at the case display you *know* about it.

That is, by looking at this case display you learn almost immediately as much as the eye can tell you about the knife and its maker. There are still library facts to be learned, though, so the museum director has added a written label to his display for you to read and learn more from. He puts down when and where the knife was made and found; out of what kind of stone it was ground or flaked; what other artifacts were found with it (if there were any); how old the knife is (if that has been determined); what the blade was used for, and who (man or woman) used it.

For instance, if the director is displaying a special type of knife, like the crescent-shaped stone blades of the Eskimos, he will explain that knives of that type are made by men but that women use them to scrape the meat off sealskins before tanning them. If the blade is a sharp-pointed knife, meant to be used by a man in hunting, that information will be included on the label. If you study the label and display *together,* you can learn the important facts about that particular knife, as far as we know them now. That's a little hard to believe, isn't it? All the same, if you really pay attention in a museum, you can learn as much as if you read many books, and learn it quickly and pleasantly. By the end of a short visit, you should know as much about that knife in the case as if you had actually held it

in your own hand. Don't try to hurry with this kind of looking. It can only be done slowly.

So when, in this round of the archaeology game, we talk
about going to a museum, we mean going to *read* the museum
—going there for the purpose of finding out what is on display and what each artifact means. We don't mean aimlessly
walking around, upstairs and downstairs, or running and sliding in the halls, or smearing chewing gum on the glass fronts of
the display cases. (Somebody does one or all of these things in
every museum in the United States every day.) We are talking
now about using a museum for its real purpose: to find out
about the lives and customs, and most especially the materials
and methods of manufacture, of other peoples, living and dead.
We mean learning how other peoples' lives resembled, and
how they differed from, our own.

In many museums there are displays of the artifacts made
and used by the earliest Indians when they began to settle down
and stay put—in one place or another, all across the country—
at the end of the wandering time. By then these Indians and
their forefathers had looked at most of the continent, and decided what region they liked best. These were Indians of a
later time, not the real, first wanderers we talked about in the
last chapter. But neither were they the truly settled peoples of
a later period. They are sometimes called the People of the
Archaic Period—the men of the ancient past.

Wherever archaeologists have had a chance to search all over the United States, they have found some traces of the Archaic peoples. Evidence of the lives of the Archaic peoples have been discovered in the mountains of New York and Virginia, not to mention most of the states between those two. The evidence extends through the Rocky Mountains and up to the Columbia River basin, and then, with gaps, even farther north. Usually it is easy for a trained eye to recognize the traces of the Archaic peoples when it sees them.

We don't know which areas of the continent are oldest in occupancy. Reports of new finds are published almost every year. Until more of them have been issued, and compared with one another, many of our most important questions must remain unanswered.

So far, some of the earliest specimens of human manufacture that have been found north of Mexico are certain easily recognizable chipped-stone points. The first discovery of one—what is known as the "Paleolithic type point"—was made on the eastern New Mexico plains near the little town of Folsom. There the bones of a now-extinct form of buffalo were dug up. Embedded in one of the leg bones was a chipped-stone point.

This type point is about two inches long, made of a hard, pinkish-brown chert. In the center of each face, running from haft to point, there is a single long, narrow groove. It marks the place where one delicate flake of stone was lifted off by a single tap of the tool of a highly skilled workman. Points of

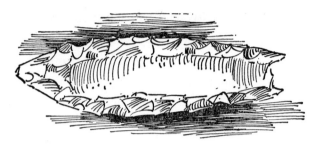

Folsom points were first found in New Mexico

the same type have since been found in places far from Folsom, New Mexico, and even farther from each other—from interior Alaska to upland Georgia, and places in between. Wherever they are found, though, these are called Folsom points. Archaeologists usually name specimen types for the sites where they are found, or the cultures with which they are associated, just as botanists, paleontologists, and entomologists name plants, fossils, and bugs for their friends.

Even if the Folsom people weren't the first Americans, they set the pattern for all Americans since their time, for they were great travelers. Other early stoneworkers left their characteristic implements in many places. One discovery was made in Yuma County, Colorado, and the type point, therefore, was called a Yuma point. In the Yuma points, the worker controlled his tools and materials so that a finely rippled surface was produced in the same kind of stone that the Folsom artists used. We mention these two particularly because they are types of such fine workmanship that you can recognize either one instantly, as soon as you see it. Other ancient point types worth looking for in your museum are the Clovis, the Sandia, and the Scottsbluff, and we could list many more.

But there isn't time or space here to describe all the different types of prehistoric points, or to tell where and how each was found. For the present we will even ignore the question of how old the points are. Probably, like other artifacts, they were made first at one place, then at another, and the range of ages for Folsom and other points is as wide as their geographic distribution. So far, we cannot say with certainty which site is the oldest.

Ideas—like new ways of making stone tools and weapons—need time in which to travel—to be perfected and taught and learned. Think of how slowly the use of electricity for power is still spreading around the world. There are many parts of North America without electric lights even now, though people who live in large cities may have trouble believing that statement. And ideas and objects travel faster and farther today than they did in any earlier period of human history.

Now we'd better move on, and leave the Folsom and other ancient points to the experts who are still studying them. Let us go on to the cases with the work of the Indians of the Archaic Period. The label tells us that this material came from caves, and, just as an example, let us use material from a cave in western Arkansas, which is displayed in the museum of the University of Arkansas.

Looking at the case, one question pops immediately into my mind. Is this the kind of material I expected to find, or has the museum director been preparing surprises for me? I expect the rest of you, wherever you live and in whatever museum you are looking at a display of Archaic life, feel a good deal the same way.

Well, naturally, by this time we would expect to find stone tools and weapons, and sure enough, there they are. Knife blades, which we can recognize easily by this time, with their three-to-six-inch length, are grouped in the display with tiny, sharp points, possibly made for blowgun darts, for they are less than an inch long. Beside the points are curve-bladed—some semicircular, some almost round—scrapers for cleaning meat off hides. In the case we also find stone axes or hammers, grooved three-fourths of the way around, so they can be securely fastened to wooden handles. The handles themselves, of course, have rotted away long ago. There are also some hammer stones without grooves. These could have been clutched in a worker's hand and used to pound with, as we sometimes hold stones to crack nuts when we are out of doors. The flaked points and blades are made of pink or brown chert; the ground hammers and axes are of gray granite or greenish-black diorite.

Besides the stone tools, we find fragments of food in the

case. There is a little pile of wild seeds—wild mustard and certain grasses furnished these people with a part of their food, according to the label. There's another little pile, this one of wild-plum stones. The soft fruit has dried up and blown away long ago, but the hard pits are left. A fistful of charcoal fragments tells us that the Archaic people used fires for cooking, heating, and light; it even tells us what kinds of wood they burned. There are a few broken bones left over from the rabbit the family ate for dinner the night before they moved out of this cavelike bluff shelter high above a stream. Lying off to itself, and looking as if it had been scraped clean with a stone knife before it was thrown away, is a deer's shoulder blade. The man of this family must have been a good hunter. He used his stone points, and perhaps walked long distances, to find and kill game for his family's food.

The mother must have worked hard, too, to gather the wild seeds and fruits, to dry them, and to store them away. What did she store her surplus food in, so she could keep it for the winter's needs? The case label tells us that most of the food fragments were found in a hole scraped in the wall of the bluff shelter—a cache, it is called. There was another cache in the cave floor, between the back wall and the fire pit. The family liked this cave, then, and meant to come back to it another year. Perhaps they stored food here from one season to the next, year after year, and returned to the cave at regular intervals. They must have lived a little the way some city families do now, spending the winter in town and the summer in the mountains or at the seashore. Perhaps this shelter was the Indians' winter home. A map drawn on the label shows us that the cave faces south, so that in winter the sun slants into the cave mouth and warms the whole dwelling.

That cache in the cave floor was not just a hole dug down into the earth. After the pit had been hollowed out, it was carefully lined with tufts of wild grass, twisted together into loose bundles. These formed a padding between the food and the damp earth, and prevented the seeds' spoiling or sprouting. Over the pads a mat was spread, one that had been plaited from the split stems of wild cane. There is a good-sized fragment of the matting left, lying on the floor of the case as it once lay on the cave floor. The little piles of food are displayed on it, to show more clearly how the mat was used.

So this Indian mother, all those thousands of years ago, was a good housekeeper. She stored winter food for her family as well as she could without a canner or a deep freeze. She waded in the swamps downstream from the shelter to gather the knife-sharp cutting stems of the wild cane, handling the stalks carefully in order not to hurt her hands, so she could make a mat to line her storage cupboard. She was a deft worker; the mat is beautifully made. The shiny outer surfaces of some strips of the wild cane alternate with the dull inner surfaces of others, so the herringbone pattern of the plaiting will show clearly.

This woman loved her family. She worked hard to make their home a pleasant place, to make beautiful things that were meant to be used every day.

What else can we figure out about the Archaic people by looking at their belongings in this museum case? There's a pile of little bark-fiber strings heaped in the corner beside the weapons. A square knot is tied in the center of each scrap, joining two cords together. What in the world would anyone do with all those knotted strings? Nothing, of course, as they are now. But just suppose you could see them all spread out on the ground, in the way the hunter saw them when he first knotted the strings together. Then the broken ends beside the knots would join string to string to string. Presently you would have a fine-meshed net laid out and covering a large space.

There aren't any fishbones in this case, so our first guess—that this was a fish net—is probably wrong. There *could* have been fishbones, and they *could* have rotted away, of course. But the rabbit bones are as fine as many kinds of fishbones, and the rabbit bones are still there. . . . That's what they used the net for! They stretched it between two trees or bushes, or fastened it to stakes driven into the ground, and drove the wild rabbits into its meshes. Then the hunters killed the game with clubs. The method must have been more certain than shooting at the small game with blowgun darts or arrows, if they had them. It was much more accurate than hurling a javelin at a rabbit with an atl-atl, or spear thrower. It's much easier to make a net and club than many small darts and shafts to attach them to.

If the Archaic people made threads and strings and mats and nets—as they evidently did—did they also make cloth? Well, yes and no. There are some fragments of twisted rabbit-fur strings in other museums, like the cords that modern Indians have been known to use in making woven rabbit-fur blankets. There are also a few nets with feather shafts fastened into the knots and loops of the meshes, so the feathers would have overlapped one another on the surface of the fabric as they had on living birds. These specimens are not evidence of true cloth as we are familiar with it, and I don't know whether we ought to count them as cloth or not. Some archaeologists do, and some don't. Let's leave that question unanswered for the present.

At least we can be comfortably sure that the Archaic people didn't go barefoot all the time. Here is a lone, lost sandal plaited out of wild cane, like the mat. Its bark string still dangles, waiting to be tied around a wearer's ankle. It is a good big sandal, probably made to fit a grown man. The Indian father must have walked a long way in it, to have worn clear through the sandal sole. Perhaps the night he brought the rabbit home—the night before the family moved to their summer home in the low lands, where they would be nearer the water and the wild-plum thickets—the man's wife plaited him a new pair of sandals to wear on the trip. That would explain how this one came to be left behind on moving day. We'll never know what happened to its mate. Maybe a pack rat carried it away and left this strange, dark, shiny galena pebble in exchange.

This Indian housewife certainly wasn't wasteful. She made little bags of deer hide, one each to hold red, yellow, and white earth paints for make-up. She made a comb for her hair. It,

A man's cloud-blower pipe and tobacco pouch

and the paint bags, are still in a larger sack. She probably thought of it as her make-up kit. She used the bits of buckskin she had trimmed from the edges of a hide to make the bags, instead of cutting up a big new piece of deerskin.

Another bag is lying on the mat, a little away from the woman's things. Dried, powdered leaves spill from its open mouth onto the plaited mat. This might have been the man's smoking sack. He carried it with the pipe that lies beside the pouch, a pipe that really looks more like a cigar holder than it does like a modern pipe. It is made of a section of a deer's leg bone, wrapped and bound with deer sinew to reinforce it. Most of the sinew has dried and cracked and flaked away long ago, but there is still a little of the heavy muscle binding left to show that once the whole pipe was bound. Pipes like this, which are usually called cloud-blowers, are still occasionally smoked in Indian ceremonials, because it is believed that a style so old must also be sacred. A roll of tobacco, willow, or other leaves is thrust into the outer end of the pipe, and the smoker holds it in his mouth, his head tipped back to get a good draw.

One of the cave-family children must have lost this necklace —a string of red and black seeds, pierced with a fine, sharpened bone, perhaps, and strung on a grass thread. We think of girls right away, of course, because we are used to seeing girls wear necklaces. But even today some Indian men and boys wear necklaces, so this ornament *could* have belonged to a boy. Boy or girl, the child who lost the necklace couldn't have been more than six years old to have been able to slip this string around his neck.

Now, before we go on to the next case in the museum and play another round of the archaeology game, perhaps it would be a good idea to make a short list of the things that, as far as we know now, the bluff-shelter people lacked. We will make only a short list, because, if we included everything that can be thought of, the list would be too long to carry around the museum with us. Here are a few of the items we can include:

The bluff-shelter people were not farmers. Their vegetable foods came only from wild plants.

The bluff-shelter people had no domesticated animals except dogs, so they relied on wild game to give them a balanced diet.

The bluff-shelter people were not fishermen. Or, if they were, there is no evidence of the fact.

The bluff-shelter people made no pottery. They used grass pads and wild-cane mats to line pits for storage, instead of mouseproof, fireproof pottery jars.

The bluff-shelter people had no measuring lines or measuring devices of any kind, yet they were skilled craftsmen. Whatever they made, they made well. They probably were far too busy to be fine artists only for the pleasure that artistry gives. There is nothing in this case that was made only to be looked at for the luxurious enjoyment that can come from looking at a beautiful thing. Even the string of wild-seed beads, the sandal, and the face paints were a part of their wearers' clothing, and were not intended to be enjoyed for themselves.

As we said to begin with, this particular case contains material from an Arkansas bluff-shelter. Everything in it can be matched, in one way or another, from sites in Utah and Colorado, Oklahoma, Missouri, Tennessee and the Carolinas, Illinois and Wisconsin. As time goes on, more Archaic sites probably will be located, and we *may* eventually discover that they extend literally from border to border and from coast to coast. Already we can guess that the Archaic people lived in most parts of the North American continent.

Now, let's go on, and try another case in another museum. Playing the museum game this way, on paper, has its advantages; we can pick out any museum and any display we are specially interested in, sure that what we describe can be matched—sometimes very closely—in other museums in other parts of the United States.

Here are some things to look for in playing the next round: garden and field crops; evidences of bows and arrows; cradleboards, or hammocks for carrying babies; jewelry, pottery, and fine and finer basketry; and, above all, real cloth, which means that weaving had been invented.

Before we start looking for all this advanced technology, though, we ought to take a little time to talk about an Indian culture which looks simple at first, but gets more complex as we study it. It is so highly specialized that you can hardly believe that people would want to live that way.

4 Farthest North

IN ONE WAY THE ARCHAEOLOGY GAME IS LIKE CHECKERS OR CHESS. You must remember all the moves your opponent and you have made, while at the same time you consider all the possibilities for future moves. In archaeology the opponent is not a person, but time and weather working together as a team, so you really have to be prepared for double trouble.

First we are going to backtrack a little, leaving the Archaic peoples of the mid-continent cozily settled in their caves and bluff shelters. We will return to the last chapter but one, to talk some more about the movements eastward below the Arctic Circle, back in the days of the advancing and retreating ice sheets, back to the times of the first wanderers.

This round, also, is played in a museum, and a good thing, too, for most of us. The subarctic is a long distance from forty-nine of the United States, and getting there can be complicated and expensive. Besides using the museum, you may decide that you want to go to the library before this round ends. Only the biggest museums in this country have all the artifacts we will discuss. Unless you live in a large city, you will probably have to rely on pictures in books to get an idea of what these objects look like. These are the work of the people of the Farthest North.

To begin with, we all know that today the farthest northerners are the Eskimos. How far can we go beyond their name? There are Eskimos in Asia and Greenland and in North America.

All Eskimos, whether they live in the Old World or the New, speak the same language. There are differences in dialects among them, naturally, like the differences in speech among modern white men in New England, Virginia, New York, New Orleans, and Montana, but the basic Eskimo language is the same wherever it is spoken. Basic English, too, is the same, whether it is spoken in Saskatchewan or Florida.

Until a comparatively few years ago the Eskimos in Alaska used to paddle across the Bering Strait in kayaks or in the skin boats they call umiaks to visit their cousins in Siberia, and the Siberian Eskimos paddled back and returned the visits. In 1955 the Eskimos in northern Canada heard such interesting radio broadcasts coming from Greenland in their own language that they invited the Greenland Eskimos to visit a group of Eskimos living in Baffinland. Greenland is a Crown Colony of Denmark, so the Danish government made the Eskimo visit an official one of good will. The trip was a great success for everybody.

That is one illustration to show how close one Eskimo group actually is to others, in customs and traditions as well as in language, today. In the good old days—say four to ten thousand years ago—they were probably just as close, perhaps closer. At any rate, it is difficult even for experts to determine on which side of the Bering Strait any given artifact was made.

Some climates make work harder for archaeologists, and some make it easier. The frozen North is a helpful climate, although you might think that the opposite would be the case. Here, where there is a natural deep freeze, objects caught and encased in the ice may be preserved unchanged for centuries. It is not easy to dig in the frozen earth of the northern tundras, but, in summer, camp sites along the ocean shores thaw enough to make excavation possible. If archaeologists can't dig, they can—and do—watch the glacier mouths near the sea, for artifacts that may have been frozen far inland and during the creeping course of centuries have reached a place where they can be recovered.

From the remains of plants and animals, trapped and frozen when the ice was forming, we know that in the last interglacial period the climate of the extreme North was not so cold as it is now, and certainly not so cold as it was during the time of glaciation. Great tree ferns once grew in tropical abundance where there are now frozen plains that barely sustain inch-high arctic flowers for a couple of weeks in midsummer. The tree ferns, in their day, furnished food for woolly mammoths. And the mammoths, in their turn, furnished food for the hunters who were the ancestors of today's Eskimos.

Unfortunately for the archaeologists, although some of the mammoths were preserved in the glaciers that formed after the earth tipped on its axis, the men were not. At least, no human remains have so far been found in association with frozen mammoths. The people who died before the Ice Age began had probably been buried in the once-soft earth of the tundras. Then the earth was frozen hard and buried beneath ice and snow, and the bodies have never been recovered. But it was nature, not men, who had buried the mammoths. Some of the animals had been stuck in the mud and died near streams that later became glaciers. So when a glacier reaches the sea, breaks to pieces into bergs, or melts, it is possible to recover mammoth remains. The modern Eskimos carve jewelry and souvenirs from this ice-fossilized ivory.

Within the bodies of some mammoths stone points have been found. Some of these weapons are Folsom points, or some very similar. When the first Folsom-chipped point was discovered in Alaska, you can imagine the talk and excitement that started up among the archaeologists! Some learned scientists even went so far as to suggest that one of their colleagues was playing a joke on them: he had brought a point from New Mexico and hidden it in Alaska to confuse everybody else. Later, when other Folsom points were found in the far North, it was plain that this was no joke. Men had hunted now-extinct woolly mammoths and extinct buffalo with the same kind of weapon.

In addition to the Folsom points, some very fine ivory carvings—usually made from walrus tusks—have been discovered

Eskimo carving of a bear made from walrus ivory

by archaeologists working in the Arctic. Most of the ivory specimens are rather small, and the carvings have surface decorations of fine, engraved lines. We usually speak of them as carved pieces with surface engravings, and this is a good place to mention that often ancient and modern Indians use more than one type of decoration on a single artifact.

On the whole, archaeologists still know little about the Arctic in comparison to its vast size. We must combine our knowledge of modern peoples with what the artifacts made by their ancestors can tell us to form a clear picture of the ancient men and their daily lives. And we must keep hoping that more artifacts will be discovered to complete our understanding of these people.

Of course we can be sure that at any given point in geological time the people of the far North kept busy. When the weather was warm, they were fully occupied making weapons and tracking (and sometimes, we think, trapping) mammoths. After the extreme cold period began, the people must have worked even harder to gather food for each year during an extremely short summer hunting and fishing season. Almost all they have left us are the fragments of the tools and weapons. Only a few of their ivory carvings may have been worn as charms, jewelry, or ornaments on clothing. We cannot even be too sure about that.

So, in order to learn as much as possible about the early arctic hunters, we must turn our backs on the archaeology section, and pass on to the ethnology department. Ethnology is the study of living peoples, and in the cases in this part of the museum we can find displays of the work and art of the modern Eskimos. By studying the Eskimos of the twentieth century, we may be able to learn more about their ancestors.

A striking case display in the ethnology section of the museum shows us in miniature, for example, how Eskimos build temporary winter shelters, using blocks of snow for bricks and water, quickly frozen to ice, for mortar. There are also photographs in the case which show how this snow house, or igloo, is laid out by the man of the family. He holds a knife with a long, straight blade in his hand, and makes a circle with its point at arm's length from his body, turning in his tracks as he traces its circumference. You might say that he uses himself as the stationary arm of a draftsman's compass, with the knife point for a pencil. He can't lay out a very large floor space by this method, but the area will certainly be sufficient for overnight shelter on a hunting or fishing trip. An igloo can also serve as a temporary shelter while a family builds a larger, more permanent home. This photograph, incidentally, supplies an answer to one very important archaeological question: why have so few house ruins been found in the far North? If igloos are used for shelter—even temporarily—in winter, and skin tents such as we see in another picture are used in the summer, we cannot expect large or extensive house and village sites. By analogy, if the ancient Eskimos lived as their modern descendants do, they would have left few traces of their occupancy. The summer's sun would melt away some of the winter dwellings. We know that modern Eskimos often live in tents in summer, following the game herds across the tundras and shifting when their food supply shifts, or settling on the shores of inlets and streams to catch fish and hunt sea mammals. Their ancestors probably did exactly the same things.

There is an ivory snow knife in the ethnology case. The

fine engravings on its handle look enough like ancient ivory carvings almost to have been the work of the same man. We must be on the right track in interpreting the lives and customs of ancient men by the lives of contemporary dwellers in the same region.

On another case shelf there is a modern Eskimo cooking lamp. At first sight it looks like a bowl carved out of soapstone, which is a fairly soft, dense material. The difference between the lamp and a true bowl is that a tongue of the stone has been left projecting from the rim of the bowl to its center. In this case the end of the tongue has been carved to represent a seal. This tongue holds the wick of twisted grass or seaweed above the melted seal fat which fills the bowl and provides fuel for cooking and lighting. In a country where the only wood is driftwood, and where the coal deposits lie too deep below ground to be mined without special equipment, the Eskimos burn oil. They render down seal blubber and walrus fat, and then strain the connective tissues from the melted grease. What is left is a clear oil which will burn with a clean, almost smokeless flame in the open lamp. The fuel can also become an emergency food supply; if the family runs low on other food they can always drink the lamp oil, as we do corn and peanut oils.

And here, in an adjoining case, are the fur garments worn by the Eskimos—the loose-fitting, parka-hooded, slipover jackets or shirts made of sealskin, the soft sealskin trousers, and the high boot moccasins that the Eskimos call mukluks. No more effective garments for keeping warm in cold weather have ever been devised. Our armed services and the designers of winter sports clothes in our cities still copy Eskimo fashions. We do not know for a certainty, but it is highly probable that the clothes of the ancient Eskimos looked very much like those that their descendants wear.

We can even guess that the religion of the prehistoric Eskimos was like that of their modern descendants. We find carved ivory handles, like the handles used on modern Eskimo drums, wherever men lived in the ancient North. Today the Eskimo priest-doctors, or shamans, attach these handles to membranes of transparent seal intestines, and use them to accompany their prayers and religious songs and dances. Probably the long-ago shamans did exactly the same thing.

We have already mentioned that the ancient Eskimos were hunters and fishers. We cannot be sure that their sleds and boats looked like those used by the Eskimos of the twentieth century, but it is a safe guess that they did. Probably even the earliest Eskimos used dog teams to draw their sleds, as did the first Eskimos the white men met in the 1700's.

In this kind of archaeology we are working backward, as you can see. The method is called "interpretative" archaeology, for it means interpreting the past by our knowledge of the present. Interpretative archaeology is not so exact, it does not give us as definite information as some of the other methods that will be described later in this book. Even an expert hesitates to rely on interpretative archaeology alone; he is on firmer ground if he can support his interpretation with other facts—and artifacts.

And for the beginner in any field, the safest and surest method of learning is by observing closely the objects before him. Guessing is better left until later, until he can make informed guesses and will admit that they are guesses. All the same, interpretative archaeology can furnish him with leads and ideas and suggestions, whether or not to spend part of a too-short field season looking for house ruins in an area where the people often lived in snow houses or tents.

That is the reason for discussing interpretative archaeology now, at the beginning of this book. We will have to combine some of it with the other methods we use as we study different regions, and so it has been explained here.

Always remember that interpretative archaeology is a pair of pliers, not a crowbar. There are certain things it will not do, so don't rely on it alone. It can and does furnish a starting point for your work, and leads you on to more reliable methods.

5 How Artifacts Reach Museums

SO FAR, WE HAVE SPOKEN AS IF MUSEUMS FIRST CAME INTO BEING and then operated, spontaneously and automatically. It's been a little like saying, "There's the museum. Go and take a look at it; come back and tell us what's in it; and that's all there is to the whole business." Of course starting, equipping, and maintaining museums isn't as easy as that. Nothing worth doing ever is.

Almost two thousand years ago, in classic Rome, there were some fine museums. They contained displays made up of artifacts which the Roman legions had brought home from the barbarian nations they conquered, and wanted to show off to the Roman people. They went on the assumption that to a Roman citizen, anybody else, anywhere else in the world, was automatically a barbarian.

These Roman museums were usually attached to temples—

actually, they were parts of the temples—and the artifacts stored in them were officially offerings from the successful generals of the legions to the Roman gods and goddesses.

At a later period in European history, during the Middle Ages, kings and great lords had private museums. These were built for the same purpose that the Roman museums actually had been constructed: to show off the goods and treasures the ruler had captured from his enemies. And still later, when the men of the Middle Ages began to see that the treasures had a value in beauty besides their money value, the first true art museums were constructed. These buildings housed the sculptures and paintings of some of the greatest artists Europe and the Near East had produced up to that time, but still the buildings remained the private treasure houses of kings and nobles and great churchmen. Some of these museums were also intended to be used as tombs, and again others were erected to serve as churches or cathedrals, but in fact they remained treasure houses of art, and they were certainly museums in the sense that we use the word today.

Indeed, some of the finest collections of American Indian artifacts are still parts of the great treasure houses stocked from the conquered New World. In Spain, Austria, and in the Vatican museum there are unequaled examples of Indian art still to be seen. If it were not for such collections, our knowledge of the early Indians would be even less complete than it is.

For even now more people think of museums as storehouses

than as institutions of learning. A museum thought of as a book—in fact, as a whole library of artifacts—is a new and surprising idea to many people. Yet, if we stop to think about it, teaching museums have been around for centuries. There certainly was one in Paris in the mid 1600's. And, interestingly enough, that one was an Indian museum.

That collection was planned and gathered at the time when the French were conquering Canada, the North Atlantic states, and the Missouri-Mississippi drainage. In one sense it was a conqueror's museum, like the other early storehouses we have mentioned. As each company of French explorers set out for the New World, its leaders signed a contract with the king of France. One standard clause in the contract pledged the explorers to send back to Paris samples of the artifacts produced by the Indians who lived in the regions they would explore and conquer. The clause was included to make sure that the future rulers of Old and New France could know something at first hand about the lives and crafts of their subjects living beyond the seas. Each dauphin, it was hoped, would study Indian art along with American geography.

But don't forget that those were busy days in both hemispheres. The final result of all the pressure of business on the rulers of France was that most of the sealed leaden chests containing the dauphins' collections were stored away in the attics of the Tuileries Palace in Paris, and then forgotten. Then came the French Revolution, and with it the end of the kings and queens and dauphins of France; then came Napoleon Bonaparte; then all sorts of other political changes took place. The sealed leaden chests simply got lost in the shuffle.

So they stayed where they were, safe, if forgotten, until the 1930's. Even then all the chests were not opened. Very little of the material they contained was taken out and put on display. And, sadly enough, just after the chests had been rediscovered, World War II began. From then on nobody had time or money to spare for museums until peace had been signed and declared, and the country had settled down again.

Then, at last, a new museum of ethnology was built in Paris —the Museum of Man—and the dauphins' collections found a home. Now all the people of France, and many of the people of other parts of the world, can see and enjoy one of the greatest collections of New World art in existence; it no longer belongs to a single lonely prince.

All right; there we have one way to get a collection for your museum. Be an emperor, a king, or a general. Conquer other nations, and take the best parts of their art as your tribute. Bring your loot home and build a marble palace around it, making sure that you explain that it is meant to be an offering to your gods. This is an exciting, dramatic way to found a museum all right. Nowadays it just isn't practical.

A better method is one that many museums in this country and abroad have used since about 1800. It is still being used today, as far as that goes. You rely on gifts from people who are interested in the museum and its collections, and who want to contribute to its development and success. Through the generosity of these donors, beautiful and valuable objects often are given to the museum, and everybody is pleased. The givers are happy because they can be sure that the museum will give their treasures the best possible care. The museum director and his staff are pleased because the gifts enlarge the museum's collection and increase its value. And the museum visitors are happy because they are given an opportunity to see and enjoy objects too rare and precious for anyone to hope to procure for himself.

From the average museum director's point of view, there is one drawback in getting all his specimens as gifts. Some people who present gifts to museums are well informed; they know the history and identity of the artifacts they are giving, and they can supply both to the museum. Other donors do not know precisely what they are giving. Then the value of the specimen is automatically lessened. If the museum cannot give the public some information about each artifact in its collection, it is not doing its full job.

A great deal of staff time and work can go into identifying gifts that have reached the museum without accompanying information. Sometimes the object in question must be sent away to be studied and examined by an expert before it can be identified. It has happened that the donor said that what he was presenting was one thing; the museum director believed the artifact to be something else; and the expert, when he was consulted, had an altogether different idea of his own. In such cases more time must be spent on identification, and the object may be shipped from expert to expert or held out of the collection to be shown to each authority who visits the museum, before its identity can be established.

Some few lucky museums have purchase funds, and are able to buy artifacts for their collections. Although this is undoubtedly a good way to acquire a collection, it is still an unusual one. At best museum purchase funds are usually small. If someone comes into the museum with an object he wants to sell, he may be disappointed when he is told the museum is unable to purchase it. Perhaps the funds have run out, or perhaps the museum has several similar articles in its collections already, or perhaps there is not enough information accompanying the specimen to make it of use to the museum's public. Many museums actually make a policy of *not* buying specimens from individuals. Instead, they make all their purchases through regular dealers in art and display collections. By having such a policy, and by always following it, the museum director can be protected against charges of favoritism and unfairness. At best he may be forced to choose between a beaded belt and a new fossil, and, while the director decides on the basis of what the collection needs most, even this is not always fully understood. A few museums have tried out a policy of asking for competitive prices—like an auction in reverse—for specimens they plan to buy, but even this method is not generally satisfactory to the people outside the museum.

Sometimes the question of collection need is settled quickly because the owner of the fossil or the belt asks more for it than the museum purchase fund contains. Often prospective sellers to museums are surprised to learn that the prices they have set on their treasures are too high for the museum to pay. For an expert—or an inexpert friend—to have said that a particular article is the only one of its kind and should be in a museum means, to these people, that the object is worth a lot of money in itself. But a remark like that can also mean that the specimen has no price. We all know what a loaf of bread or a bottle of milk is worth. There are many bakers and milkmen, so it is not hard for us to set fair prices. But when there is only one thing of any kind in the whole world there is no comparative basis for setting its price. The object is, quite literally, priceless. How much it is worth to any given museum depends entirely on how much that particular museum needs that particular specimen.

In the United States there are many museums, some great and some small. A small museum is often forced to specialize— to concentrate on collecting only one kind of material—because it lacks the space and funds and staff that are necessary to build a large general collection. On the other hand, a large museum, especially an old one, may have a general collection which contains many specimens that duplicate each other. In that case, only a small part of the collection can be put on display at any one time. There are museums which display nothing but baskets, for instance. There are other museums which try to show how baskets were used by their makers and formed parts of their lives. In such displays, other artifacts can be included, to emphasize the uses of the baskets.

Often a large museum will find that it is overstocked in some fields and has almost nothing to display in others. Then, usually, some of the surplus specimens are offered for sale or trade in one of the regular museum journals or newsletters. Often museum directors meet at conferences, or by accident or arrangement, and work out trades among themselves. Some museums have listed duplicate specimens for sale in newspapers or hobby magazines, so that private collectors might have an opportunity to purchase them.

In a later chapter we will talk about community and school museums, especially about how they can be set up in a small space by a few volunteer workers. This is not the place to go into it, but remember that there are many such museums. Remember, too, that if you want to, you can participate in setting up a museum collection, whoever you are and wherever you happen to live.

Many university museums, as well as a few general ones, conduct their own field work as a means of obtaining specimens. They send out field research parties, with a trained archaeologist to direct each group of students. These parties put what would otherwise be their summer vacations into the hard work of procuring specimens for the museum's displays. This is an important and necessary phase of the museum's training program.

And let me emphasize again that museums are as much interested in securing information about specimens as they are about the specimens themselves. Neither is complete without the other. One thing explains the other. When two artifacts are discovered together, and a third object is discovered near by, each one explains the other two. Association is one of the most important things to be learned from field work. We will keep on saying so over and over again as this book continues, I warn you.

In order to be sure they get every single bit of available information about every single specimen, archaeological field parties must work slowly. Sometimes a museum sends field parties back to the same location—or site—year after year after year. Each one continues the work from the point where the last field group was forced to stop.

Many archaeologists make a point of never excavating an entire site if they can help it. Instead, they dig a part of the site—enough to yield significant information for study purposes—and leave the rest of the area unexcavated. They know that archaeological methods, like all other techniques, are constantly being improved. Therefore, it is a good thing to leave part of the site to be worked by someone who has learned

a more advanced technique than the one the present archaeologist knows.

New groups of workers are almost sure to have new materials
to work with, for example. Archaeology and its methods
changed almost overnight when plastics and their uses were
discovered. Work that had been done slowly, painstakingly,
and with great risk with plaster in 1930, was accomplished
easily, quickly, and safely with plastics in 1934. (Well, that's
overnight for archaeology, anyway. What are four years when
you're in the habit of thinking in thousands?)

Later on there will be a chapter about techniques and methods. In a sense, this is a how-to-do-it book after all. But before
we go any farther, let me give you the one unbreakable archaeological rule. When in doubt—*don't*. Wait until you can get an
archaeology expert to advise and direct you.

6 Where East and West Part Company

NOW, LET'S GET BACK TO THE PREHISTORIC INDIANS. LET'S LEAVE the museums for a while and start observing again.

In a previous chapter we said that the remains of the Archaic people or peoples are found in widely scattered locations in the United States and Canada. Wherever the remains are found, the list of specimens includes most of the same artifacts. We have suggested that many of the general resemblances among the Archaic groups are the result of the peoples' having lived so long ago. In their day and time specialization had not developed in the way it did in later periods.

It was not until the early Indians began to select environments, and settle down to living in one kind of place or another, that true specialization began. Differences in artifacts can often be traced to differences in the natural surroundings of the people who made them. If you live in a region where workable stone is abundant, then you may make many tools and implements of stone, although they *could* be made of other materials. If your surroundings provide you with wood or cane, or if there are large game animals in the region so you can obtain strong long bones to work with, artifacts that might otherwise be fashioned from stone may be made of the other materials.

In this sense, it was because of what their homelands did or did not provide that some Indian groups developed pottery and weaving and agriculture. Others did not make these inventions, but became hunters or fishers. Their art forms reflected their daily life, as did the art forms of the agriculturalists.

On page 49 of *Indian Art of the United States,* by Frederick H. Douglas and René d'Harnoncourt,* there is a map of the United States and Alaska showing where the North American centers of population were before the white men came. This map also shows you in capsule form the specialized arts of the peoples of the different regions. It is no accident that the population centers of the prehistoric peoples of this continent were in the same general locations as are our own major cities.

People everywhere need the same basic conditions if large populations are to develop and to occupy an area. There must be space for many families to live; soil that is fertile enough

* New York: Museum of Modern Art, 1941.

The Cross Timbers divide East from West

to produce crops that will support many persons; and easy access to trade routes connecting the different groups.

As you look at this map, you will notice that right down the middle of the country, in the space between "The Painters of the Southwest" and "The Sculptors of the East," there is a big blank area, which apparently was unoccupied in prehistoric times.

Then, if you compare this map with an ordinary road map of the United States, or with a map from a school atlas, you may think at first glance that this blank space coincides with the valley of the Mississippi River. We naturally think of great rivers as convenient dividing lines between population groups, especially when we know that these people relied on their own two feet for transportation.

But, as it happens, the Mississippi wasn't the dividing line between East and West in prehistoric America. In fact, the Mississippi River was the main highway of the prehistoric Indians, as it is one of our major transportation arteries today. As we know, the Indians had boats and canoes, so the river served rather to draw tribal groups together than to separate them. Artifacts on the east and west banks of the river alike were made by the prehistoric sculptors of the East. This is true for the river's whole length.

The real dividing line between eastern and western groups of Indians was about two hundred miles west of the river. Here there was—and still is, for that matter—a band of thick, stunted timber. It stretched from the Gulf Coast of Texas on the South, northward through Texas, Oklahoma, and Missouri, until it reached the southern fringe of the Missouri Ozark Mountains. There the woodlands frayed out, and the uplands became the barricade along the eastern margin of the Great Plains. From the time the first white explorers tried to get through it, this timber belt was known as the Cross Timbers—because it *cuts across* the country.

Unless you happen to have seen a section of the Cross Timbers, it is hard to believe that a band of stunted woodlands could stop anybody, particularly the Eastern Indians who were famous as woodsmen. But we should remember that the famous Indian woodsmen lived far to the north and east of the area we are describing, between the Atlantic Ocean and the Great Lakes. In that section the trees grow in open forests, and there is room to move around between trees.

The Cross Timbers are quite a different matter. The Cross Timbers are in a class all to themselves, as woods. The main

The Cross Timbers are still with us

tree growth in this belt is blackjack, or scrub oak. Blackjacks are low-growing trees, with their first branches sometimes projecting no more than a foot or two above the ground. The branches, and the trunks from which they grow, are twisted and gnarled, and the branches seem to interlock, joining tree to tree to tree for miles. Blackjack wood is tough. It is hard to chop through with a steel axe, and it must have been almost impossible to dent with a stone one. Growing in among the blackjacks of the Cross Timbers, seeming to tie them together even more closely than their interlocking branches, are several different kinds of tough vines. Some species have wickedly sharp thorns. They seem deliberately to unwind themselves from the tree trunks, to fasten into your clothes and hold you back when you enter the woods. Other species of vines have no thorns, but are as tough as the blackjacks. It is almost impossible to cut your way through them unless you are willing to whittle away at one vine at a time. And, most important of all, most of this tangle of plant life contains too much moisture to burn easily. Forest fires are practically unheard of in the Cross Timbers; they can't get started.

There are rivers flowing through the Cross Timbers from west to east. We naturally wonder why, if the Indians were able to use the Mississippi River as a waterway, they couldn't do the same thing with these smaller streams. The answer is that the rivers crossing the Timbers are seasonal streams. In summer the water shrinks down between the banks; sometimes the water goes underground and the stream beds become quicksands. At such times it is impossible to travel upstream by boat or canoe, and equally impossible to walk along the stream beds. Many of the banks are steep, overhanging bluffs.

In spring and fall, the seasons of heavy rains in this area, the Cross Timbers rivers contain water, but they flood. The streams rush down so fast, on their way to the Mississippi, that they cut their banks deeper and deeper, and are unsafe for boats and canoes to travel either upstream or down.

The earliest white explorers west of the Mississippi heard about the Cross Timbers from the Indians, and tried to cut a route through them with metal axes. The attempt was defeated by the toughness of the growth. After the Louisiana Purchase, explorers who wanted to see the new part of the United States were forced to go around the Timbers at their north end, and then turn south, to reach the Spanish settlements in New Mexico and Arizona. That is why the Santa Fe Trail crosses the Oklahoma and Texas panhandles from St. Joseph, instead of going directly across the middle of either state from Fort Gibson or Nacogdoches, both of which were settlements on navigable rivers, and nearer to Santa Fe in miles than the Missouri settlements.

The Cross Timbers are still with us. Roads have been bulldozed through them, and trees have been blasted out with explosives, but there are still plenty of Cross Timbers left on either side of the pavement. If you travel U.S. Highway 66 between New York and California, you will have the Cross Timbers on either side of you from about Tulsa, Oklahoma, to beyond Oklahoma City. You will also cross the Timbers on other east-west highways north or south of 66.

On either hand you can see how the blackjacks still grow

thick and twisted and strong. The vines bind the trees together from one side of a wide belt of bright-red earth to the other. Even when the land has been cleared it is relatively infertile. Very few people, even today, try to make a living farming in the Cross Timbers. The Permian Red Beds, from which the blackjacks grow, however, are known as markers for some of the rich oil deposits of the continent.

Only recently archaeologists have begun to search through the Cross Timbers for traces of early occupants. They have concentrated particularly on the banks of the rivers and the tributary streams, where it would have been possible for the Indians to make a way across country. The archaeologists have found indications of the Archaic peoples on the banks of the creeks and smaller rivers, and undoubtedly more will be found as time goes on. Perhaps other artifacts were washed off the banks and lost in the streams in the floods of long ago.

From now on it should be clear that whenever this book talks about Eastern or Western Indians, we mean Indians east or west of the Cross Timbers. The Timbers will serve as our dividing line—the blank space on our map.

It should be perfectly clear that in gathering together and working out this information about the Cross Timbers, we have played another round of the archaeology game without even thinking about what we were doing. We started with what seemed to be a hole in the map. Then we tried to find out why the hole was where it was. We examined written and published archaeological maps to learn if anyone had produced information about people who had once lived in the area. We found there were reports about sites located in the Cross Timbers, and that the woodlands were referred to now and then in reports on other sites. Archaeologists had described locations east and west of the Timbers, and what at first seemed to be accidental finds within the wooded belt. We know now that those scattered camp and village sites were no accidents.

Next, we checked the lack of archaeological evidence against state historical records. We went through Army survey reports, records of the early railroad surveys, and the biographies and letters of white explorers from the time of De Soto until the 1850's. Finally we referred to the maps published by the United States Geologic Survey. This government agency publishes maps that show each section of the country, almost inch by inch. From the maps we could learn that the Timbers still exist, and what their present extent is.

To finish this book work, and to make doubly sure, we consulted archaeologists who live in Oklahoma. They told us what the woods are like today, and of the few scattered finds that have been made along the Cross Timbers streams.

But before I finish, I want to add something else to your knowledge, a personal thing. Personal memories are often important to archaeologists because they can furnish leads and suggestions for future work.

From the time I began to study anthropology I wanted to study sites in the Cross Timbers because when I was about eleven years old I lived on a farm in the blackjacks. My brothers and cousins and I explored along the creeks and among the woods, and learned at first hand all there is to know about thorny, tangled vines and scrub-oak thickets. In that way I gathered information that I have been able to use since I grew up, and that I have also been able to pass on for other people to use. At the time, of course, all we thought about was how lucky we were to have woods to play in.

The rivers were the highways of the Indians

7 The Craftsmen of the Northeast

USUALLY WHEN WE THINK OF THE ATLANTIC STATES TODAY, or of the northeastern area of our country generally, we think of it as the great manufacturing center of our life. In the same way, we think of it as our great center of business and commerce.

It would be stretching our archaeology pretty far to say that the early inhabitants of the Northeast were leading businessmen and manufacturers. All the same, much of our information concerning these prehistoric Indians is derived from the fine, craftsmanlike way they manufactured their tools and implements. We have large quantities of these artifacts in some museums, together with the utility pottery the Indian women of the area once manufactured.

In referring to the Northeast in this chapter, we mean the

area running south from New Brunswick, Canada, through the New England states, and beyond, into New York, New Jersey, and Delaware. Through this area there are deposits of a fine, dark-colored, dense slate. This is an unusual stone for Indians to have worked in; it cannot be chipped or flaked like quartz or chalcedony, or some of the other stones that were used for making points in Archaic and later times. Slate must be ground down, with fine wet sand or with sandstone, if it is to be worked at all. And, by the way, this statement is equally true in regard to granite. Perhaps grinding became an important industry to the early Northeasterners because slate and granite were more abundant in their territory than other stones.

Probably the prehistoric Northeastern Indians worked in wood and bone as well as in stone, but the artifacts they must have made from these materials have not survived for us to see. A damp climate and extreme cold have combined with the passage of time to destroy them. When we examine the stone tools we see that many of them are axes or hammers, others are gouges or chisels, and still others plainly are adzes. These Indians obviously made excellent woodworking tools, which must mean that they had wood to work in. In addition to the tools, they made ground slate spear points and knives, delicate and tapering in shape, but surprisingly strong.

Now, flaking stone is quick, comparatively easy work once you get the knack of it. An experienced craftsman can turn out a knife or a point in a few minutes, while you watch him.

Grinding stone, on the other hand, is a slow process. It takes more patience than most of us possess even to think about grinding tools from a piece of stone of one kind by rubbing it against a piece of stone of another kind. It must have taken still more patience to go ahead and do the job after having thought about it.

Because grinding stone is such slow work, the craftsmen of the Northeast probably saved it for winter work. We know that northeastern winters are long and severe even now. People who live in cold country spend a lot of time indoors. So we can be safe in saying that the early Northeasterners, whatever they did in the summers, had plenty of winter working time. Probably they hunted and fished in summers, laid up a year's reserve of foods, and then concentrated on their craftswork.

Practice makes perfect, it is said, and the tools of the prehistoric Northeast look as if much time had gone into practicing stone grinding, for they are perfect. Not even a modern toolmaker, with all the precision instruments and fine measuring devices that are available to him today, could turn out more careful or accurate work. Each edge is fine and straight; the taper of each instrument is as true as if it had been gauged with a micrometer. When you think that the Indians must have worked on these tools by firelight during the winter months, and that they had to sight along those fine-drawn edges and bevels against the flicker of open flames, you realize what great craftsmen they were.

All the tool forms made and used in the ancient Northeast

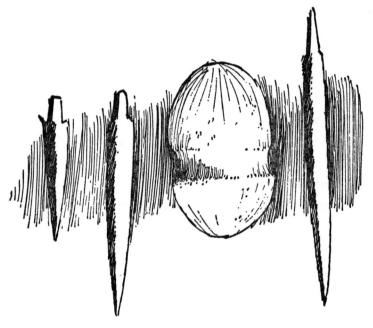

Ground slate precision tools from the Northeast

support our theory that these instruments were used in working wood. They were probably employed in making boxes, masks, and other ceremonial objects. The instrument-makers would not have put such a great amount of time into producing artifacts for which they had not found a practical use.

The same thing is true of the weapons the Northeasterners used in hunting. There was plenty of game to be found in the northern woods; they are among the great hunting areas of the world even today. Moose, caribou, several kinds of deer, wildcats, wolves, beaver and otter, and, of course, game birds of land and water, were all to be found there.

The Northeastern Indians were also fishermen. And their country is still as famous for its fishing as it is for its hunting resorts. Along the Atlantic Coast some Indians may even have had canoes that were large and stout enough for deep-water cruising. They were able to explore the bays and the offshore waters for cod, haddock, and other fish. In rough weather the Indians could collect shellfish along the shores, and probably this was one job the women and children did in all but the coldest weather.

Here in the Northeast we are able to say precisely when prehistory, or archaeology, ended, and history in our sense of the word began. We have written records of the first encounters of white men with the tribes of the Northeast—with the Narraganset, Wampanoag, Mahican, Piquot, Montauk, Massachuset, and some others. These were the first tribes that the Pilgrim Fathers encountered. Among the Mayflower Company there were many educated men who kept careful records of each day's happenings in this strange new land.

The *Mayflower* anchored in Plymouth Bay in 1620, as you probably know. From the day the anchor splashed over the side of the boat, the written history of the Northeastern Indians began.

At first the white men wrote of the Indians as their enemies. The early entries in the accounts emphasize the Indians' scanty clothing, their face paints, their weapons, and the fear that the Puritans felt of attack from the "painted devils."

Later, when the climate and soil proved to be unsatisfactory for raising the grains and seeds that the colonists had brought from England, they began to think and write differently about some of the Indians, at least. Massassoit and his people taught the white men how to plant corn, beans, and squashes in their small cleared fields. They showed the newcomers how to put a fish into each garden cluster, so that as it decayed the plants would have needed fertilizer. We know something about these and other planting customs of the Northeastern Indians for the best of all reasons: the white men had to learn Indian methods of agriculture in order to survive in the new country.

As was the case in many other parts of the New World, agriculture was a woman's job among the Northeastern tribes. The men had full-time employment in hunting, fishing, and manufacturing. Although they were probably too polite to say so, the Indians must have thought it very strange to see the white men working in the fields and gardens and their wives staying indoors. Of course, Indian housekeeping was simpler than that of the whites, although in those days the difference was not so marked as we might assume it would be. The Indians lived in plank houses with built-in beds along the walls, and with a central fire pit in each dwelling, near which the woman of the household kept her cooking utensils in a restricted area that would correspond to a kitchen cabinet. The chief difference between the furniture of a white and an Indian house—in that time and place—was that the white people sat on stools or benches and the Indians sat on mats and skins laid on the floor. Plank walls, pounded-earth floors, smoke holes, and windowless structures were otherwise much the same.

I often think it is too bad that the Northeastern Indians didn't know how to write when they and the white men first met. It would be interesting to know if the Indians thought the white women had a pretty easy time of it, with nothing but housework to do and clothing for their families to make. It would be interesting, too, to have their comments of the differences between the white men's religion and their own from the early Colonial Days until the Revolutionary War.

As it is, we have only one side of the fascinating story. History was written by the white men although it was lived by both peoples. Often they chose to record the customs that seemed ridiculous to them, or that shocked them, or even things that they thought were downright wicked in the way the Indians lived. When the writers included comments the Indians had made about white people, they wanted to show how "rude and incivil" the Indians were, and how little they understood the "Higher Scheme of Things."

For instance, the Pilgrim Fathers had openly left England to seek a land where they could worship God in their own way.

Religious freedom was the most important factor of their lives, the cornerstone on which all their plans for the Colony and its future rested. But it had to be their kind of freedom, their way of worship, and their God. When the Puritans encountered a wholly new kind of worship—like that of the Indians—they simply wrote in their diaries that the Indians worshipped devils, and that ended that matter. They added no details as to the number of the devils, the way in which the Indians worshipped them, or what they had to do—if anything—with the Indians' belief in an afterlife. For this reason we know nothing about the religious beliefs of the Northeastern Indians at the time the Plymouth Colony was founded.

We will never know how these Indians traced descent in their families. We cannot learn how they named their children, or what toys they gave the children to play with. It is too late to find out how young couples married and set up their homes. We will never know how members of families felt toward one another, or what their terms of affection and kinship were. The Indians' ways were *different* from those of the white men, and for that reason the white men thought the Indians' ways were wrong. This kind of snap judgment is easy, and we all of us make it at one time or another. In this case, before the white men and the Indians could find out that it is possible to bridge the differences between men's customs, the Indians had largely been eliminated. The Puritans brought with them colds, whooping cough, and other European diseases to which they had some immunity, but to which the Indians did not.

A sure proof to the white men that the Indians were devil worshippers was their custom of smoking tobacco in pipes. The Puritans said that a man *must* be in league with the powers of evil in order to draw smoke from a burning herb into a tube, down into his lungs, and then exhale a dense white cloud. And the time that the Indians wasted fashioning their pipes was surely additional proof that smoking was a thing of evil! Nobody ever recorded what the Indians thought of having their incense plants uprooted from their gardens, their laboriously wrought incense burners shattered on the ground.

Speculation of this kind is fascinating, but it is also fruitless. Let us get back to more concrete objects, to things we can hold in our hands, for after all this is a book on archaeology; it is a book of science, not of science fiction.

Archaeologists have learned, by studying hundreds of different peoples who live in many parts of the globe, that when people have agriculture, the women usually make pottery. This was the case with many of the Northeastern Indians. Compared with some of the pottery we shall describe later, when we discuss Indians in other parts of this country, the pottery of the Northeast was not very exciting to look at. Most of it was a dark ware, usually a dirty gray in color, although a few almost-black vessels have been found in the southern and western parts of the area. They may have been made there, or they may have been traded in.

Often, when the northeastern wares are examined under the microscope, it is possible to see that fragments of ground-up shell were worked into the clay. Potters today use a substance called "grog." In either case, the material is added to spread the dense particles of the clay apart, and to allow the pottery to dry and fire more evenly. Some prehistoric wares show a mixing of sand or even of tiny stones; others contain ground-up pieces of broken pottery; a few have been found that contained strands of grasses or weeds. Mixing another substance with the clay in this way is called "tempering" it. We speak of shell-tempered, grit-tempered, sand-tempered, sherd-tempered, and vegetable-tempered pottery, according to the nature of the added material. And we are going to speak of all of them quite often from now on.

In the western part of the geographical northeastern area, from the Finger Lakes of New York westward to the Great Lakes, and perhaps beyond them, lived Indians who were different in many of their customs from the tribes who lived along the Atlantic Coast. They were Iroquoian-speaking. The coastal tribes seem to have spoken a series of related languages that we know today as Algonquin.

The Iroquoian women developed a specialized type of pottery all their own. The main body of the vessel was globular, practically a ball in shape. The upper part of the vessel—the

Iroquois women developed special pottery shapes

shoulder and rim—was formed in a square collar. Often these collars were decorated with simple patterns of straight lines, or were ornamented with small clay masks, applied to the outer surface of the vessel before it was fired. The decorative lines, also, were cut into the clay while it was moist.

Pottery wares into which lines have been cut before firing are called incised. Other methods of decorating moist clay vessels are by pinching the surface with the finger tips or denting it with the thumbnails or with the point of a stick; by pressing it with pieces of cloth or basketry to give it a textured surface; by wrapping a flat paddle with cloth, cord, or other material and beating the surface of the vessel with it; by wrapping a piece of string around a stick and rolling it around the vessel to leave its mark on the damp clay surface, or by simply pressing a piece of cord into the clay over and over until the whole vessel is covered with its marks. These are all important methods, not only because they accomplish their original purpose of decorating an otherwise plain and uninteresting piece of earthenware, but also because they tell us what kind of string, basketry, cloth, or netting a particular group of prehistoric people made and used. It is possible to learn a great deal about prehistoric textiles by studying the marks that have been made with them on pottery.

Surfaces of vessels can also be decorated after the clay has dried and hardened, before or after it is fired. Paint is the decorative medium we think of first, of course. The Eastern Indians used earth paints, and we shall discuss them more in detail later on, in connection with the groups that made the greatest use of them. It is also possible to make fine line decorations on pottery by scratching them with a sharp point into the hard surface produced by firing. Such wares are called engraved. Sometimes earth paints were rubbed into the lines engraved on pottery to give the decorations additional emphasis and beauty; sometimes the lines were left plain.

Like most other American Indian pottery, that of the Northeastern tribes was made by the coil method. When a woman started to make a vessel, she mixed dry clay and dry, crushed tempering material. She added water to the combination, and then worked and kneaded the mixture between her hands until the materials were evenly distributed and the air bubbles had all been worked out. If even one pocket of air, however small, were left, it would expand from the heat of firing, and the vessel might fly to pieces. At best the jar would be warped and twisted out of shape; at worst, its explosion might shatter every other vessel the potter had placed in the kiln with it.

When the potter felt sure her mixture was smooth and solid, she patted out a disk of it that was as big around as the base of the vessel she wanted to make. She might place her clay pancake in a gourd bowl, a mussel shell, a basket, or the bottom of an old broken bowl to support it while she worked, or she might place it on the ground before her. In either case she then took another piece of clay, worked all the air bubbles out of it, and coiled it around the edges of the first piece. She added other coils above the first one, always being careful not to join their ends in the same place, but to stagger the joins, like those in the courses of brick in our buildings, so there would be no danger of the pottery's drying with a crack up one side. When the potter had raised the walls of the vessel to the height she wanted, she took a smooth, curve-edged piece of shell or wood or old pottery and dipped it in water. With this scraping tool the woman worked around and around the vessel, taking off the surplus clay where the ends of the coils joined, and smoothing the outer and inner surfaces of the pot until the ridges of the coils had disappeared.

Even when she had finished all this work, the woman was not ready to fire her vessel. First she set it out in the shade where it would dry slowly and evenly. Pottery exposed to the sun dries quickly and unevenly, and is likely to warp or crack. Making enough pottery to keep their households supplied must have been endless work for the Indian women, but, like their men, the women had great patience. They worked steadily but slowly, and they obtained almost perfect results.

We have already suggested that a knowledge of textiles, like that of pottery, occurs among people who have developed agriculture. In the severe climate of the Northeast, very few textiles survived to our day; most of them rotted away like the wooden artifacts. The fabric impressions left on northeastern pottery tell us that these people made both twined and plaited cloth, nets, baskets, and mats, as their descendants did in historic times. Since we find tools to be used in tanning and working skins, we are probably safe in assuming that the Northeastern Indians wore skin clothing in prehistoric times, although no examples of such garments have come down to us.

Probably the most interesting single fact about northeastern archaeology is that there is any. Not only has extensive work already been done in the area, it is still going on, and, although the whites have occupied the country so long, new discoveries of archaeological sites are still made in the northeastern area. Our knowledge of the early Indians of the region will undoubtedly continue to grow for years to come.

Almost every time a large northeastern city expands, for example, and trenches are dug for new water mains or sewer pipes, or foundations for new buildings are excavated, archaeological specimens may be found. If you happen to know where an excavation of some sort is going on in your own neighborhood, try to get permission from the contractor to watch the dump heaps. See if the workmen are digging up occasional bits of broken pottery or worked stone or pieces of shell. If you do notice fragments of artifacts on the dumps, try to get further permission from the contractor to take the scraps to the nearest museum (there are lots of museums in the northeast) so that a staff archaeologist may have an opportunity to study the specimens.

Watching excavations to see if fragments of the past can be discovered in the course of contemporary jobs is called "salvage archaeology." In many ways, it is one of the most important archaeological procedures in use in our country.

In fact, the United States Park Service, some state governments, and even certain oil companies, employ salvage archaeologists as staff members. These men go out with road construction or pipe-line crews, and watch the work in progress and the growing dump heaps for archaeological material. Specialized training is necessary for a salvage archaeologist, and the more of it he has, the better job he can do. Still, anyone who is observant can take part in this phase of archaeology. Keep your eyes and ears and—above all—your mind wide open. An important find in salvage archaeology may be waiting for you not more than a block from your home.

8 *Meanwhile, Far to the Southward*

WE SHALL HAVE TO GET BRACED FOR A CONSIDERABLE GEOGRAPH-
ical and mental jump when we go from the Northeast to the
Southeast. We shall have to move backward in time, too. True
prehistory ended and written history began in the Southeast
almost a hundred years before the same change took place in
the Northeast.

The first white men who encountered the Southeastern Indians were Spaniards. They had already conquered and occupied most of the Caribbean Islands, Mexico, and much of South
America. In the islands, some of the Indians described to their
conquerors a great land that lay to the north. The Spaniards
set out to find—what? A larger Cuba? A richer Mexico? Another Europe? Certainly treasures of gold, silver, pearls, and
spices like those they had taken from the southern lands. With

the troops went missionary priests, as eager for treasures in saved souls as the soldiers were for wealth.

Ponce de Leon was the first to sail to the northward, searching, so he said, for a fountain of eternal youth. He was followed by Hernando de Soto, who landed on the Florida peninsula in the spring of 1534 with a much more material objective. De Soto started out, probably from the vicinity of Tampa Bay—his exact landing spot has never been identified—to find an overland route into Mexico. On the way, he naturally conducted a survey of the country he crossed and claimed all lands for the king of Spain.

As the leader of a well-stocked military expedition, De Soto made sure that exact records of the country and the peoples who lived in it were made and kept up to date. In consequence, we have three firsthand descriptions of the lives of the Southern Indians in the early sixteenth century. After all, whether they knew it or not, those Indians had become Spanish subjects the moment they were seen by De Soto and his followers.

Remember, this was only thirteen years after the Spanish conquest of Mexico, which took place in 1521. De Soto and his companions had had an opportunity to learn from Cortez and his followers how useful it was to know all they could learn about the Indians whose territory they were going to occupy. For that additional reason, De Soto ordered that great care be taken to make accurate observation of the Indians and their lands.

So, even if no archaeological work had been done in the southeastern states, we would know that these Indians were not only agriculturalists primarily, but that they also hunted and fished. We would know that the people lived in walled or stockaded towns, with their fields of corn, beans, squashes, and tobacco laid out beyond the village enclosures. Usually these towns were located on the second terrace above a stream. The houses were safe from floods, but the people did not have to go far to get water when they needed it. The planted fields usually were situated on the first, or lower, terrace, between the town and the stream. There, if the land were flooded by rising water, it would also receive enrichment from the silt deposits the rivers brought down. Or if there were a long dry spell, the fields could be watered by bringing jars of water from the rivers to the gardens.

At all periods in southeastern prehistory, from Archaic times until the landing of De Soto, and even afterward, the Indians ate great quantities of shellfish. Along the Florida Coast and the banks of some of the inland rivers, for instance, they left huge mounds of discarded shells. Some shells were used as sources for pottery temper, or were pierced to make beads, or carved to make ornaments, or ground down to be used as bowls, but still the supply of unused shells greatly exceeded the demand. Some of the oyster, clam, or mussel shells probably contained pearls, for fresh- and salt-water pearls have been found in archaeological excavations in the Southeast, but those great shell heaps cannot be explained even by a thriving pearl industry. The Indians liked to eat shellfish, and that's all there was to it.

From the Spanish records we are able to identify the Natchez, Creek, Chickasaw, and Choctaw groups of villages with certainty. Some of the other tribes have never been satisfactorily identified with their living descendants. In some cases this is because of differences in pronunciation among the Indians, the sixteenth-century Spaniards, and ourselves; in others it must be because the living descendants have themselves died out. Many, many southern tribes became extinct soon after their introduction to the first white men and to European diseases.

From the Spanish records it is clear that the Natchez, Choctaw, Chickasaw, and Creek Indians especially had a strongly coordinated social and religious organization, and that this was true, although in lesser degree, in other tribes and confederacies of tribes.

These Indians were governed by chiefs who had inherited their offices, and who often were as powerful as smaller European rulers of the same period. There was a series of social classes in these tribes, ranging from the chiefs and their families at the top down to the slaves at the bottom. In those days the slaves were frequently Indians of other nations or tribes, who had been captured in town raids or in battles. Most of the hard, heavy work was performed by the slaves, so their masters had ample time to devote to astronomy, philosophy, govern-

Stone grave figure, Etowah Mound, Georgia

ment, and the arts. Their carvings in wood, bone, stone, and shell have survived, as have specimens of the fine pottery that was made by the women. Some of the greatest prehistoric works of sculpture found in North America were executed in the Southeast.

From the archaeologist's point of view, perhaps the most fascinating single feature of the life of the Indians of the Southeast was their religion. Not a great deal is known about it, but what we do know is tantalizing.

Although the Spaniards were usually so careful about their record-keeping, they were no more accurate or helpful about Indian religions than the Pilgrim Fathers would be in their later day. The Spaniards, too, wrote that the Indians worshipped devils and ought to be burned at the stake for doing so. That is almost all they put down about it. In this they are no help to the modern archaeologists at all.

But, fortunately for human knowledge, less than a hundred years after De Soto and his men had come and gone, the French in their turn explored the Southeast. They voyaged down the Mississippi from the Canadian Great Lakes in Indian-made canoes, and on the way they watched the Indians closely and noted down whatever they saw. The first great French explorer who reached the northern boundary of the southeast area at the Ohio River was Father Marquette. He had his say about devil worship, as all the other early white men had. However, Father Marquette was an unusually observant and thoughtful man. At least he took the trouble to keep field notes about the different varieties of devils and ways of worshipping them that he encountered.

Southeastern Indians carved stone bowls in bird forms

Two later French explorers, Bernard de la Harpe and Etienne le Page du Pratz, followed Father Marquette's trail for a time, then turned aside to visit many of the Indian tribes of the Deep South. They were not missionaries, but deputies of the French king, so they had less to say about devils and more about the people they encountered. It is thanks to these two men that we know at firsthand what the place of religion was in the lives of the Southern Indians. We are told that some Southeastern tribes decided when to wage wars and against whom, by their need of prisoners to sacrifice to their gods.

Throughout the Southeast—all the way from the Atlantic Coast to the eastern margin of the Cross Timbers; as far north

and south as from the Ohio Valley to the Gulf of Mexico—
are scattered evidences of the Indians' way of worshipping.
Throughout this vast region during one period of its history,
the Indians built up mounds of earth, with sloping ramp sides.
On the crest of each pile they erected temples, usually of wattle-
and-daub construction.

Temple-topped pyramids were built by Southeastern Indians

To build a structure of this kind, the Indians pounded up-
right poles into the comparatively soft earth at the top of the
mound. Then branches of willow or stalks of wild cane were
woven in and out through the gaps between the poles. This
basketwork construction was the wattle part of the building,
and it was daubed over, inside and out, with damp mud, usually from a nearby river bottom. The French explorers wrote

that sometimes the dried mud of the walls was painted over with pictures and decorative designs. If only one or the other of the two explorers had copied some of the decorations and so had left us a record of southeastern mural painting at the beginning of historic times! But so far, no painted walls have been found intact, and no copies were left, so we can only guess what the decorations looked like.

It seems a little strange that the Spaniards, who had seen Aztec and Zapotecan temples in central and southern Mexico, barely mentioned the mounds raised by the Southeastern Indians. While there is nothing to show that the prehistoric Indians of Mexico and the prehistoric Indians of the southeastern United States were the same people, or even that one group knew of the other's existence, they shared many common traits. The building of temple-topped pyramids was only one of them; there were similarities in costumes, agriculture, and even in their use of feathers in ceremonies. It is quite possible that the Spaniards were not so much impressed by the southeastern temple mounds as the French were simply because the Spaniards *had* already seen or heard about the great stone structures in Mexico, and earth mounds looked poor and mean to them.

Several times, now, we have suggested that written history can help to make archaeology clearer. In this case, the situation is reversed. From excavations that have been made in different parts of the Southeast, we learn that some mounds were used as cemeteries, while others were temple bases only. Probably

*Carved shell gorgets link the Indians of the Southeast and
of Mexico*

only important priests and chiefs, and perhaps the members
of their families, were buried in the mounds. Perhaps, too, some
slave captives were sacrificed when a great chief died and were
buried with him.

We know that the Aztecs, like the Southeastern Indians,
waged wars to obtain prisoners to sacrifice. Here is another of

those tantalizing gaps in our story of the people who once lived on this continent. The Aztecs sacrificed prisoners annually, at midsummer. In the Southeast, prisoners were certainly sacrificed when important men were buried. But is it even remotely possible that one of those important men was himself a prisoner, guarded and cherished as a living representative of the gods for a whole year, and then "returned to his brothers," as was the Aztec custom? We simply do not know, and we probably never will know.

At any rate, it is safe to say that just before the white men invaded their country, and for a short time afterward, the Southeastern Indians laid great emphasis on death. There are vessels from mounds in widely scattered areas that are incised or engraved with designs of skulls and crossbones. It was a great period of sculpture, and some of the statues made by artists of this time are stone figures in the round of men and women, dead and prepared for burial. In Arkansas, particularly, clay jars modeled to represent dead faces were made. Since the specimens of this rather gloomy art now in our museums come from burial mounds, perhaps the statues and vessels were intended as death offerings. This, too, resembles a form of Aztec religion, a cult of death, presided over by its own grim gods.

The early accounts written by the Frenchmen describe the elaborate burial rituals of some of the Southeastern Indians. Bodies were exposed on scaffolds to the sun and air, until the flesh dropped away from the bones. Then the bones were scraped absolutely clean of flesh by certain older men or women who let their fingernails grow long and kept them sharpened for just this purpose. When each bone had been thoroughly cleaned the skeleton was ready for burial; either the bones were packed into a large pottery urn, or laid out as they were in life (articulated) on the earth, or bound together in bundles with bark string before they were buried in the temple base. From some excavated skeletons it seems likely that human or animal sacrifices were made at the time of burial rather than at the time of death, for often only one skeleton in a grave indicates that it is being reburied, so to speak, and the other bodies seem to have been buried soon after death.

And with the bodies of their great men and women the Southeasterners laid away what were for the time and place really vast treasures. We have mentioned pottery and statues that seem to have been made especially for grave offerings. Fine textiles were used to wrap the bodies or bones of the dead; there were offerings of jewelry and other ornaments; all kinds of valuables were included, probably, as we have said, including slaves. A little later on we will get around to a real inventory of a temple mound.

Whether they worshipped death itself, or whether they only respected their dead, the Southeastern Indians went to a great deal of trouble about funerals. We know much less about their religion as it applied to life—whether they had gods of planting and harvest, gods of rain and fertility, gods of light as well as gods of darkness. Probably they did. Probably these gods were more important during the early years of tribal history than they were at its ending. If we wanted to be imaginative and non-scientific about the matter, we could even say that it seems as if the Indians had some preknowledge of the fate that was ahead of them; that in making a cult of death the Southeastern Indians were preparing for their own funerals.

Now, the trouble with making the kind of general statements we have here is that it is so easy to find an exception for each such rule. If we say that these things were *generally* the case in the Southeast, some scientific archaeologist will certainly come along next week and point out a specific place where none of these generalizations can be made to apply. And he will be perfectly right in doing so. There *are* exceptions. Not every southeastern mound was a temple mound, or a burial mound, or even an artificial mound. All I can do now is tell you to go and read the reports about specific sites, or clusters of sites, or river drainages, if you want to know more about this culture, if, as a culture, it fascinates you as much as it does anybody who has ever been fortunate enough to work with it. Because I have worked a little in the field of southeastern archaeology, I know how great its fascination is. I also know that anyone who wants to contradict any of my generalizations should certainly be able to do so.

Choosing one particular southeastern site to write about is a risky business. But I am going to describe the temple mound at Spiro, Oklahoma, partly because I worked there and partly because the whole story of what happened at Spiro is a perfect archaeological example of how *not* to do it.

First of all, there shouldn't have been a large temple mound at Spiro; it was too far west. Spiro lies in the Arkansas River bottom between the Ozark Mountains in Arkansas and the Cross Timbers in Oklahoma. All the great temple mound sites were much farther east at such places as Moundville, Alabama, Etowah, Georgia, and Cahokia, Illinois. Spiro certainly lay at the extreme western margin of the mound-building area.

The Spiro mound was constructed on the second terrace above the Arkansas River. Indeed, so much earth was scooped up from the soft river "bottom" to be used in building the mound that there is still a slough, or shallow pond, between the river and the mound's base. Elsewhere, for acres around the site, the earth is flattened—ironed over and smoothed out by many seasons of plowing.

The story of how even a portion of the Spiro mound came to be scientifically excavated is a long one, and probably all of it will never be known or told by one person. Part of the story of the Spiro excavation can be written down, though, and I think this is the place to do it. Let the tale serve as a warning to everyone with a hobby interest in archaeology. Just because you expect to find some Indian artifacts, *don't* go out and start digging.

Somebody—usually a teller of the Spiro story—says it was a farmer plowing and getting ready to plant corn on the leveled land between the mound and the slough in the Arkansas River bottoms. Like most of his neighbors, the farmer hardly noticed the mound. It had stood there ever since the neighborhood was settled in the middle 1800's, and there were fine big trees and a tangle of bushes growing all over its slopes. If the farmer thought anything at all about those two hillocks of earth, joined together by a saddle lower than their crests, which formed the compound mound, he probably thought that they made up a natural hill of a rather unusual shape. So he plowed a curved furrow—scalloped, actually—around the base of the hill, because he didn't want to drive his mules up and down the slope, or try to plow around and around the slanting sides of the hummock.

Suddenly the blade of the plow—the plowshare—struck something hard in the ground, and the farmer stopped plowing to look down. He had hit a reddish, rounded piece of stone —and there are no red stones that occur naturally anywhere near Spiro. You have to travel about a hundred miles in any direction to find them.

The farmer stopped in his furrow. He bent down and scraped away the earth around the strange stone with his hands. Finally he revealed a stone figure, like nothing else he had ever seen before. It seemed to be a combination pipe and incense burner. The figure was too large and heavy for anyone to hold in his hand to smoke, but the ashes crusted in its bowl were certainly tobacco ashes. For a little while the farmer speculated whether the pipe might have been smoked by a giant—it was all so surprising that anything seemed possible. Later he was to learn that these "great pipes," as they are called, were smoked by setting the pipe on the ground, and attaching a hollow wild cane to its outlet hole.

Naturally the farmer saved the pipe. Naturally he took it home to show to his neighbors. But that came in the evening. All the rest of the day he continued plowing and wondering. And after the neighbors had seen the pipe, and admired it and wondered how it got where it was, the farmer thought about it some more. Much later that year, after the cornfield had been plowed, planted, cultivated, and harvested, the farmer went back to the mound. He brought some friends with him, and they helped him clear the ground at the base of the hill. When the bare earth was exposed, the men began to dig.

Well, you probably have got the idea by now that if there is anything in the world that scientific archaeologists are opposed to, it is indiscriminate digging. It is all very well for an archaeologist to be handed a stone pipe someone else dug out of a hole in the ground. The pipe is a work of art, and the archaeologist can enjoy looking at it as much as anyone else would. But, aside from its beauty, a lone pipe means very little. If the pipe had been found beside a skeleton, or laid beside what was left of an altar, and *that* information were available with the specimen, then the archaeologist would know what he was looking at besides a piece of sculpture.

Unfortunately, the first diggers at Spiro had never been told this fact of archaeological life. They had no idea of the importance of associations in understanding and interpreting artifacts. All that the first explorers of the Spiro mound knew was that they had a handsome red-stone pipe, and they guessed that there might be others like it buried somewhere in the earth of the mound. A cousin of one of the diggers had told them that collectors in the East would pay good money for "Indian relics" other people dug up. ("Indian relics" is a careless and inexact expression. Archaeologists use it only in quotation marks, as slang.)

The first Spiro diggers were amateurs—what archaeologists usually refer to as "pothunters." There are amateurs and amateurs, and not all of them are pothunters by any means. Pothunters are the kind who dig up "Indian relics," and what they call "Indian heads" or "arrowheads," regardless of size and shape and purpose, with the full intention of selling whatever they excavate. They don't know any better, but, as you can see, they *could* learn.

These pothunters immediately chopped down the trees that covered the mound, thus committing another archaeological offense. A trained eye could have learned a great deal from them. The kinds of trees, their height and thickness, and whether they were first- or second-growth timber would all have added to the archaeologist's knowledge of the site.

With the trees down, the workers began to dig anywhere that they could stick a spade in the ground among the stumps; they grubbed out the tree roots, and hacked away the undergrowth. Most of the plant cover was dragged aside and burned. Even the tree stumps would have been helpful to an archaeologist, who could have counted their annual growth rings and formed an idea of how many years it had been since the site was abandoned.

It seemed as if the diggers struck buried treasures wherever they looked after the surface of the mound was cleared. In the first few days of work they dug up more of the great sculptured stone pipes; some beautifully carved pieces of shell; pearls —spoiled and discolored by burial, but pearls, all the same. They found fine, hard, dark, polished pottery, and some specimens that had dark-red pigment rubbed into the delicate lines engraved on their outer surfaces. They found crumbling, paper-thin sheets of embossed copper, some of it dissolved by time and earth acids so there was nothing left but a green stain on the earth to show where it had been, some of it still firm and strong. They found stone and bone and shell beads and pendants, delicately worked crystals, and great ground greenstone axes, adzes, and maces. And many of these artifacts were like nothing the diggers had ever heard of or seen before, although a trained archaeologist could have matched most of them against artifacts that had been taken from other sites.

At first the pothunters were cautious; they had found so

much more and better material than they expected that they hardly knew what to do about it. They trusted only a few people enough to show them their finds. But soon word of the discovery began to spread, and eventually the news reached collectors and dealers in archaeological specimens. A little later on, a newspaper published a story about the site. The Spiro mound became known as the "King Tut's Tomb of the Arkansas Valley," for this was not many years after the excavation of the tomb of King Tutankhamen in Egypt.

Eventually the word reached responsible museum administrators. They notified the University of Oklahoma that archaeological treasure was being dug up inside the state, and sold outside it.

By the time the first professional archaeologists visited the site, the treasure hunters had formed themselves into a mining company, and taken out a business charter under the state laws. As a company, they had leased the mound and the acreage surrounding it. They had figured out that a mining company would be the best sort of corporation for them to organize because, after all, they had to dig for whatever they found. The members of the company soon decided that digging by hand was hard work and a slow method of excavating. Instead of digging, after that, they scraped away the earth that formed the sides of the mound with mule drags, the kind that used to be employed in road construction. After a while the pothunters decided that the earth was too hard and dense even for the drags—it blunted their sharp edges, for one thing—so they drilled holes in the sides of the mound, loaded the holes with dynamite, and blasted the mound open.

You can see for yourself that these men were not primarily interested in learning the story of the long-ago people who had built the Spiro mound and buried their treasures within it. These men wanted only the artifacts that were still whole, and that could be sold. So the bones of the skeletons, the broken strings of beads, the small wooden and bone implements, the fragments of feather cloth, and the potsherds—all the bits and pieces that archaeologists could have fitted together to make a coherent picture of the past—were spread out on the dump, and before the pothunting ended the dump had been spread over the better part of an acre of land.

So many people had a share in ending the pothunting and saving a portion of the Spiro site for all of us to learn from it that we cannot begin to mention names here. The State Legislature passed a law that declared prehistoric sites were the responsibility of the state and that whatever knowledge they could yield belonged to all the people of Oklahoma. It was made unlawful for anybody to dig in prehistoric sites without first obtaining a license to do so from the Department of Anthropology at the University of Oklahoma. People who discovered prehistoric sites were expected to report their finds to the university archaeologists, who would issue excavation licenses to people who were qualified to receive them. Diggers were also expected to report on their finds and on the material taken out of them.

The University of Oklahoma, Tulsa University, and the Oklahoma Historical Society all cooperated in raising funds and finding personnel for scientific excavation of the Spiro site. The Federal Government, through its Works Progress Administration, supplied additional funds to pay laborers to work under the direction of trained archaeologists. A botanist took samples of soil from the mound and the slough, and tested the earth for buried pollens. He had hoped to be able to determine just when the mound was built. This effort failed, but he was able to demonstrate that the earth in the mound had come from the slough. A specialist in tree-ring dating took samples of wooden posts that were found in the mound, as well as samples of the charcoal that was found with some of the burials. This was done so he could compare the annual growth-ring patterns from the specimens with those of other pieces of wood taken from the same rainfall area. This cross-dating is still unfinished.

But most important of all, the whole area was searched and surveyed carefully. The method that was employed was one variation of a system that is used by many archaeologists. There is no one standard method of excavation—there are as many methods as there are sites and archaeologists to dig them. But there is a general pattern for archaeological exploration and the development of sites with which everyone is familiar.

At Spiro, the first thing to do was to survey the mound and the area surrounding it, as land is surveyed for laying out a subdivision for a city, for planning a highway, or for setting water mains and sewer pipes. The surveyed surface was then shown on maps obtained from the United States Geological Survey. Finally, the area was divided into ten-foot squares, like small city lots. Stakes were driven into the corners of the squares, marking them out on the ground, and the same squares were drawn to scale on the site map.

The horizontal ten-foot squares were next resurveyed and divided into one-foot squares, each numbered and each indicated on the site map. Then the first archaeological digging began. A test pit was sunk from the surface of the ground to a level of undisturbed earth. The place chosen was at an outer edge of the mound, but it could have been anywhere in the surveyed surface area. In this case, the undisturbed earth seemed to provide a floor or base for the earth piled above it.

This floor was called the *datum plane*. It became the level at which gathering vertical data began in this mound. From the time the datum plane was established, everything in the mound was figured as coming from so many inches above or below the datum plane. A datum plane is purely arbitrary as a general rule, and is established for the workers' convenience. It is theoretically possible to establish a datum plane five feet in the air, above the surface of the site, but this is seldom, if ever, done. Any practical level will serve as a datum plane, but,

As the trench is dug deeper, it also grows wider, a step at a time

once it has been established, it must be observed. A letter system is frequently used to show the relation of vertical squares, on a given profile of the excavation, above or below the datum plane.

With the datum plane established, the digging crew excavated a trench into the mound, working inward from the pit that had first been dug to determine the datum plane. The men in the crew worked down, taking out one level at a time, and going forward along one of the surface survey lines. As the trench grew deeper it was widened a foot at a time on either side, so the diggers had room to work in. Everything that was excavated as the trench progressed could be—and was—charted

as coming from its own lettered and numbered cube of earth
in the site. Supervisors followed the diggers to check the profile
faces of the cubes for protruding artifacts, and to make sure
the horizontal levels were maintained.

As we have said, this particular adaptation of an excavation
method happened to be usable at Spiro. It was hoped that, as
trenches deepened and profiles were revealed, additional information concerning the construction of the mound could be
gathered.

Great care and attention is required at this stage of excavation. Often artifacts or bones have decayed, and only faint dis-
colorations of the earth remain to show that any foreign substance was ever there. Sometimes a faint, light line against the
soil will show where one long bone has been dug into and
destroyed while there is still time to salvage its mate. Lenses
and strata in the profile of a trench may indicate periods when
the site was successively occupied and unoccupied, where fires
were built, where cache pits were dug to conceal food or other
disintegrated substances. Traces of wooden posts, or the holes
in the earth into which they were set, may be revealed. It is
possible, by working slowly and carefully along a profile, to
know whether burials within the site were careful or casual,
and which was which. As each changing feature of a profile is
revealed, it must be charted on the field map, to be transferred
to the master site map at the end of the day.

Usually, digging begins with shovels. As soon as any of the

traces of occupancy we have mentioned—or one of many others —is observed in the profile, shovels must be laid aside, and the work done with trowels, scoops, spoons, or brushes. When an artifact is found protruding into the face of the trench, the supervisor must decide whether to excavate it at once, or to leave it where it is for the present and to remove it later, when the trench is widened. These decisions are usually reached on the basis of the size and fragility of the object.

It is not a good thing, as a general rule, to try to dig around and under the object, loosen it, and take it out immediately. Undercutting may weaken the sides of the trench, bringing down a slide of earth and perhaps damaging other artifacts. If the artifact seems to be of very delicate material—cloth, basketry, bone, or shell—it is sometimes decided to take the risk of undercutting in order to secure that one specimen. If the artifact seems to be a good solid piece of pottery, or a stone pipe, or a piece of well-preserved shell, then it is usually left in place until it can be removed in the further course of excavation, and can be seen in relation to other artifacts near by.

If the material is very flimsy, or if a large number of small artifacts has been discovered clustered together, a matrix is built around artifacts and their enclosing earth. This method is one that geologists developed for the removal of delicate fossil specimens, and archaeologists learned it from them. First, earth is removed from the top and sides of the specimen, until it is left resting on a pillar of earth. The face of the specimen

*Carved cedar masks were taken from the Spiro sites
in plaster matrices*

is covered with tissues and then with wet newspapers, and then
bandages made of burlap soaked in plaster of Paris are wrapped
around and over the top and sides. When this layer of bandages
is dry and set, the earth beneath the specimen is deliberately
undercut and the lump is rolled over, face down, with the speci-

men protected by the tissues, newspapers, and plaster bandages. More bandages are wrapped around the newly exposed surface, and the letter and number symbols—the site location series—are penciled on the outer layer of plaster. Specimens encased in this way can be removed from the field to the museum laboratory safely and easily.

Another method, often used in preserving textile fragments, is impregnation. The earth is removed from the specimen with tablespoons and camel's-hair brushes until the whole surface is exposed. Liquid plastic is then poured over it, and allowed to dry. Perhaps several coats are used; sometimes one gives the specimen sufficient body for safe handling. The substance is then lifted directly from the ground, or it and its surrounding earth are encased in a matrix for safer handling and transportation.

The general rule in excavating is: first, shovels; second, trowels; third, spoons; fourth, whisk brooms; fifth, camel's hair brushes and small bellows. As much earth as can be removed safely should be taken from the specimen before any attempt is made to handle it in the field. Sometimes, as with skeletal material, it is often desirable to leave the material exposed and allow it to dry out throughly before plastic is applied; sometimes, again with bones, a matrix must be built around the specimens immediately, for air will destroy whatever is left of the skeleton.

As each specimen is removed from the earth, in order to preserve their relationships to each other and to avoid confusion, it is marked with the number and letter representing the cube of earth in the site from which it was taken. Sometimes each item within each cube is given a separate specimen number; sometimes a single serial number is used for the cube collection as a whole. Several small articles, such as a collection of points, may be put in a single paper bag and given a collective number; another bag may hold the fragments of a large pot and be marked with that vessel's number.

The important point to be observed in removing specimens from the dig is that each must be kept separated, and must be distinguished, in some way, from all the others. It would be silly, after all the work that has been done to prepare a site for excavation, to dump everything in one large box at the end of the day.

When the specimens are delicate, and might be easily broken by handling or by contact with other artifacts, each is carefully wrapped in tissue paper or cotton as soon as it is removed from the ground. Then each specimen is put in its own, separately labeled box. Each container, box or bag, must carry the cube and object identification.

Every artifact—its location, description, and associated objects—is entered in a field catalog as soon as it is brought in from the dig. On a big site, like the Spiro mound, keeping the field catalog is a full-time job for a trained and experienced worker. On smaller sites, cataloguing may be one part of a worker's assignment, and he may spend the rest of his time digging, cleaning, or repairing specimens. Whatever the size and the nature of a site, however, the cataloguing must be done regularly, on every day of digging. If the field catalog is not well-organized and up to date, confusion and trouble inevitably develop.

When the surface and profiles of a site have been properly mapped and charted, and the digging has been carefully done, not only every artifact, but every teaspoonful of earth can be restored to the place from which it was taken. To be able to map and reconstruct a structure is an important and necessary procedure when a mound is located in a state or city park, for instance, or when it is a well-known regional landmark. A community may want to know what is in the mound, but at the same time want to keep the landmark for people to see. In such a case, reconstruction of the mound, after the artifacts have been removed from it, is essential.

Restoration of the site was not required at Spiro. For one thing, the owner of the land, from whom the university had leased the digging rights, had asked that the mound be leveled and its earth spread over his cornfield, so plowing the area would be easier. He also, of course, had a larger area to plow and raise crops on. And, for another thing, so much damage had already been done to the mound by careless digging—not to mention blasting—that it had already been largely destroyed.

But even more important than preserving landmarks is obtaining information from a site. This is the real reason for all the painstaking mapping, diagraming, charting, and cataloguing that must be done in the field. The relationship of artifacts to each other is the most important information to be gained. Relationships are always more important than specimens.

You can easily see that work of this sort requires trained supervision. Excavation is not a job to charge into recklessly because you happen to want some "Indian relics" around the house. And in order to be sure that present and future excavation is properly done, many states have passed what are known as "antiquities laws," in order to protect the buried treasures that belong to the state's whole population.

If you will look at the table in the back of this book, you will find a list of places where you can write to learn if your state has an antiquities law, and what its provisions are. Before you are tempted to start operating a dig on your own, check on the law in *your* state. Find out who has the authority to issue a license for archaeological excavation.

Do *not* ever—wherever you live, whoever you are—just wander out into somebody's cornfield and start digging a hole to see if there are any "Indian relics" at the bottom of it.

First of all, of course, get permission from the owner of the land to dig in it. If he doesn't want you in his cornfield and you go there anyway, you can run into plenty of serious trouble. The best that can happen to you will be a bawling out. The worst could be a court trial for trespass and a heavy fine.

You are always liable for prosecution for trespassing on some-body else's land or for breaking a state antiquities law. Some-times you may have committed both offenses. Then the penalty, like the crime, can be multiplied.

Now, let's backtrack to the beginning of this chapter, and the lives of some groups of Southeastern Indians. Let's see what, if anything, Spiro has to tell us about those ways of life. This will be a harder job than the reconstruction would have been if we had discussed any one of several other southeastern sites. Admittedly, the information gained from Spiro is fragmentary, at best. Admittedly, Spiro was at the western margin of the Southeast, and probably is not an exact parallel for cultures farther to the East. Still, even under these handicaps, something can be learned about the lives of the Spiro people that will throw light on the ways their contemporaries lived.

Was there or wasn't there an inner chamber in the Spiro mound? The University of Oklahoma began work at the site in 1935. There are still plenty of people alive who worked on the excavations. Not one of them is in agreement with the reconstruction in the university museum, which shows an elaborately constructed burial chamber as the central inner feature of the mound.

Some of the surviving pothunters say they found an inner chamber when they blasted open the side of the mound; some say there wasn't anything of the kind; some say there might have been but they aren't quite sure if there was.

Judging by the size of the cedar posts and beams that have been recovered from the Spiro site, there was a structure of some sort connected with the mound. It may, however, have been the usual kind of Southeastern wattle-daub temple on the flat top of the earthworks. Fragments of dried clay, showing impressions of wattled walls on one surface, have been gathered from the site. There could have been a house, or a ring of houses, on the top of the mound rather than a single temple, on that evidence.

If an inner chamber did exist, what was it used for? Was it meant only to be the tomb of an important man? Was it a storage area? Or was the mound, originally, of the type found at Ocmulgee Old Fields, Georgia, and other southern sites, where the mound was more or less incidental covering of a council chamber, a semisubterranean house or meeting place?

Whether the mound was built originally as the base of a temple, or whether it was formed by the accumulation of earth above an underground structure, whether it was a landmark and gathering place, solid in form and without an inner cavity, it was also a cemetery. Many skeletons were recovered from the earth sides of the main structure. In most cases, the possessions of the men, women, and children of Spiro had been buried with their owners' bodies. There were fine bowls, water- and seed-bottles, and pieces of heavier, coarser utility pottery with many burials. More great stone pipes were unearthed. Shell-bead necklaces and pendants (or gorgets) of shell were discovered. There was fine sculpture in stone, wood, and embossed copper. There was delicate engraving and carving of shell. There were fragments of bark-fiber, nettle-fiber, and twisted-feather cloth, some of it still brightly colored. There were pieces of lace, scraps of bags and of sandals. And there were the pearls—we will say more about the pearls later.

Probably the shell gorgets as a group are the most important artifacts taken from the Spiro mound. They are decorated with engraved pictures of life at Spiro: dances, ceremonies, and such everyday events as two men paddling a canoe in a stream.

The line drawings on the shells are still clear. The artists engraved every detail of men's clothing and dance costumes. None of the shells, so far as I know, shows a picture of a woman or a child, which makes us think that the shell pendants were intended to be worn by men in ceremonies, rather than as simple illustrations of the life of the village.

Animal and bird life was clearly shown on some gorgets; there are some decorated with pictures of eagles, of pileated woodpeckers (a bird that is now almost extinct), of spiders, of raccoons, and of what are either terrapins or armadillos—the experts are still arguing about this one.

Some gorgets are decorated with abstract designs that may have been associated with the religion of the people. There are crosses—a design that some contemporary Indians say represents the stars, others, that it is the four corners of the world (the four directions). There are swastikas; outspread hands attached to braceleted wrists and decorated with rings on the fingers. There are winged serpents. Besides the gorgets, the Spiro people made and used bowls of whole conch shells. Some of these are carved with life forms like those on the gorgets, while others are decorated with geometric or curvilinear designs.

The Spiro people lived on a navigable river, and the canoe drawing shows that they used it. They must have been great travelers. The bowls and gorgets, and most of the shell beads, are made from conch shells brought from the West Indies or the Florida Keys. With the carved objects, supplies of unworked shells also were found. Exactly what route the shells traveled before they reached Spiro we do not know. The great conches may have been traded from tribe to tribe, passing through hundreds of hands during a period of years on their way from extreme southern Florida to east-central Oklahoma. On the other hand, expeditions may have set out from Spiro to the Caribbean for no other purpose than to obtain the shells.

How did the pearls get there? Experts have said that some of them are not fresh-water pearls but true salt-water pearls of a type that is usually found off the coast of Venezuela. Somehow, bags of the pearls got inland to the middle stretch of the Arkansas River.

It is easier to determine the travel route of the sheets of copper. The metal came from the Great Lakes region, for there is no source of supply nearer to Spiro. The black obsidian (volcanic glass) that the Spiro craftsmen used in making knives and fine points probably came from New Mexico, although a little has been found native in Arkansas. Still, the chances are that much of the stone traveled around or through the Cross Timbers on its way to eastern Oklahoma. The red bauxite, or aluminum ore, from which the great pipes were carved, certainly came from Arkansas. So did the greenstone that was ground down with wet sand to make the ceremonial maces, and the amethyst, quartz, and rock crystal which were worked to make exquisite ornaments to be worn in ceremonies or offered to the gods. These materials did not travel as far as the other things we have mentioned, but they did have to be found and brought to the place of the mound.

Curiously and interestingly enough, it seems that in many cases the raw materials, not the finished artifacts, were brought to Spiro from their places of origin. The Spiro community had its own well-developed and easily recognizable art styles. The work done at Spiro is *like* that executed in other parts of the Southeast, but is not identical with any other style.

A further curious fact about the Spiro site is that so far, although many experts have hunted carefully for years, nobody has yet found the village where the people lived. It took many laborers to build such a large mound. It was a center of worship and council for a large population during a long period of years. Usually, when an important ceremonial structure of this sort is discovered (and the number of skeletons recovered from the mound is proof that it was a center of some sort for many people), the homes and fields and other traces of community life can be identified not far away. But there is no evidence at hand to show that a large population group ever lived near Spiro.

At first archaeologists working at the site supposed that the river had changed its bed, and in doing so had washed out the remaining traces of the town. Geologists tell us, however, that while the Arkansas River has shifted its bed frequently in the last thousand years, there has been no one change great enough to destroy all indications of a village. They also assure us that there are no signs that earthquakes ever took place or volcanoes erupted in the vicinity. The Spiro village could not have been wiped out by a natural catastrophe other than a flood.

Well, what *did* happen to the Spiro people? Or were there any? Today, twenty-five years after scientific excavation began at the site, that question is still unanswered. Nobody knows.

But on the basis of our knowledge of other Indian communities, particularly those in some parts of Mexico, whose people had art styles similar to the Spiro art, we can make a *guess* that only a few people ever actually lived at Spiro at any one time. Perhaps some priests and their families were stationed there permanently to watch over the mound, and to perform daily religious ceremonies.

And perhaps those priests were artists as well as men of

religion, as were many of the monks of the European Middle Ages. Part of their time these men devoted to worship and the performance of its rituals; part of it they spent in carving and painting offerings and ornaments for their altars. If the larger population—whom, in a sense, they represented— brought the artists offerings of food and skins and feathers; of copper and bauxite; of semiprecious stones and shells and obsidian, so that the priests and their families did not have to worry about their daily bread, it is easy to understand how they and their wives might have become the great artists and sculptors and potters we know contributed to Spiro art.

In such case, we have a ready explanation for the piles of unworked shells, the lumps of uncarved stone, and the bags of raw-earth paints that have been found embedded in the Spiro mound. Perhaps the ordinary people of the village lived scattered over the bottom lands and had their farms up and down the river. They may have followed the game, traced the trade routes, paddled their canoes along the streams on fishing trips, and then returned at regular intervals to their center of worship and its appointed guardians.

Then, when the worshippers did return, they might have brought with them all the different raw materials from which the priestly artists wrought their offerings for the temple, the magnificent ornaments to be worn by the chiefs and the high priests. Perhaps . . . and again, perhaps. . . .

And perhaps, even now, as late as it is in the history of the

Spiro mound, some day a few of these questions may be answered and the speculations they arouse confirmed or silenced. We shall know, then, whether the guesses I have set down here are right or wrong or somewhere in between. We shall know with certainty if some archaeologist is lucky enough to find a similar site that has not been looted. But it is more likely that because a few people, years ago, were greedy and careless, the rest of us will lack the answers to these questions forever.

⑨ How Old Is Old?

SPIRO WAS DESCRIBED AS ONE OF THE RICHEST ARCHAEOLOGICAL finds of the twentieth century, but it is not the only mound that has produced treasures. Even with the material objects of art that were recovered, Spiro was not as important to archaeologists as it could and should have been, because the information we have about the site is still incomplete.

Actually, other mounds in other parts of the Mississippi drainage have furnished us with more, and more complete, information than Spiro has, even though they produced fewer specimens.

Earth mounds of several different types are found along the main river drainages, all the way from Louisiana to Wisconsin. Many of them were overgrown with trees, and could be mistaken for natural hillocks when the white men first discovered them. In time, someone dug into a mound and discovered it held fine artifacts—even works of art. Then, for a number of years, it was debated whether or not the mounds had been built by the ancestors of the Indians the white people themselves knew. Many people simply refused to believe it.

The first white man who wrote a careful description of a mound of any sort was Thomas Jefferson. He suggested in his paper that the earthworks must have been constructed by the members of "a vanished race." Mr. Jefferson referred to the race and its members as the Mound Builders, and the term was quickly accepted. For many years it was used even by archaeologists to refer to the builders of mounds of all types.

Mr. Jefferson lived in an age of intellectual speculation. Science then was just beginning to take the approach to natural and man-made phenomena with which we are familiar today. It was beginning then to examine ideas in the light of evidence, instead of stating a thesis and then looking for evidence to support it, as had been done by earlier philosophers. But it was still felt that a man needed a thesis to begin with—an intellectual springboard, so to speak, to start him thinking.

A great many dives into the unknowns of natural phenomena taken by Mr. Jefferson and his contemporaries seem farfetched to us today in the light of our scientific knowledge. As far as the men of the eighteenth century knew, however, it was just as safe to assume that America had originally been populated by the Ten Lost Tribes of Israel, by Norsemen or Welshmen, or by Egyptians, as by people from anywhere else. Even then, it seemed, no one thought of America's having been populated by Americans. From the first, it was assumed that the ancestral Indians got here from somewhere else, and the first question to answer was: Where? Many of Mr. Jefferson's philosophic friends speculated that the first Americans might have come from "Lost Continents," named Atlantis and Mu, which had since sunk beneath the Atlantic and Pacific oceans. There is no geological evidence, as far as we know now, to show that such continents ever existed, although there is evidence of many changes in the forms of the oceans' floors.

Of course, when you are hearing about prehistoric migrations for the first time, it is just as easy to suppose that the ancestral Indians came from the East as from the West. In fact, if your own immediate ancestors came from Europe or the British Isles, it is not only easier, it seems more natural. It is only because all the available evidence so far shows that Asia was the continent of Indian origin that this theory is the accepted one today.

There is no geological or geophysical evidence that Atlantis or Mu ever existed. No traces of early Caucasoid man, or any form of early man, have been found in the New World. Most significantly, there is a strong resemblance between materials from archaeological sites in Asia and Alaska. This is all we know so far.

So we must accept the fact that the people who built the

mounds were American Indians, and probably American Indians who lived not so long ago. Many of them existed in the protohistoric period; that is, the time when white men had invaded some parts of the country and begun writing the history of those regions, but had not reached other areas yet. Some of the builders existed after this twilight zone that is neither archaeology nor history; they were alive in the historic period, as we have seen in discussing the writers of the French histories and explorations in the South.

But other mounds are still undated. Some of the biggest, finest, and most conspicuous of them, as mounds go, have been found in the Ohio River Valley. Probably the great serpent mound in Adams County, Ohio, is the most famous single mound in the world. The body of the serpent follows the curve of the river bend for more than two hundred feet, and nowadays it stands two and a half to three feet high above the datum plane.

A few burials have been found in test pits sunk in the sides of the serpent mound. These bodies appear to have been buried long after the construction of the mound; they do not seem to be the reason for building the mound in the first place. Perhaps these are the bodies of people who came long after the builders of the mound had moved on somewhere else. No attempt has ever been made to excavate the entire mound. If the work were properly done, the serpent mound could be reconstructed, of course, but most people feel that in that case it wouldn't

The most famous mound is Ohio's great serpent

be *quite* the same as it once was. And so far, the burials that
have been excavated have not had enough associative material
to justify the risk of spoiling of a famous landmark.

The artistic and associative returns from other sites in the
northern part of the mound area have been considerably richer.
Stone carving was the field of the greatest achievements of

these people. Their finest sculptures are stone pipes. Many greenstone, limestone, or diorite pipes from the Ohio area have what sculptors of today call a "monumental quality." That means that, although the pipes actually are small, they look big. Some of them are only an inch or two long, but if they are photographed alone, without rulers or other objects included in the picture for comparison, they could be almost any size.

For instance, a famous sculpture of this type is a red-stone pipe in the form of a singing, dancing man, with every detail of his costume shown. This pipe was excavated at Adena, Ohio, and is now in the museum of the Ohio State University at Columbus. The figure is eight inches high and it weighs a pound and a half, but a photograph of it has been enlarged to make a photomural eight feet high, in which detail, proportion, and character remained as clear as in the original specimen. Photographers and artists often *reduce* pictures of artifacts at the scale of one inch to one foot, and find that the objects remain clear and recognizable in the smaller pictures. But to *enlarge* a picture of a small object and find that it does not become blurred, indistinct, and lacking in character is a different matter altogether.

There are other effigy mounds in other states than Ohio. Some in Wisconsin represent birds or turtles, and there are other serpent mounds. Some of the more northern effigy mounds have been excavated, and the material taken from them has

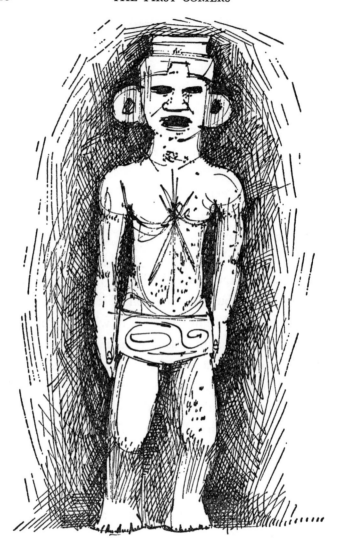

Stone pipe from Adena, Ohio

proved sparse and simple, quite different from the variety and richness of objects from the southern mounds.

Besides making the fine stone pipes in the forms of men, birds, and animals, the prehistoric Indians in certain parts of the country specialized in what are called in archaeological slang "problematical objects." That is, it is quite certain that these artifacts are objects. It is also certain that they are artifacts. The problem is: What were they used for, if anything?

The list of problematical objects is a long one, including what are called "bannerstones," "birdstones," "butterfly stones," and net weights, sinkers, or plumb bobs. The first artifacts in this list do indeed suggest the shapes of banners, birds, and butterflies without representing the forms literally. It has been suggested that they were used in games; also that they were used as atl-atl weights on spear throwers. We still have no knowledge of what they meant to the people who made them and, presumably, used them, but so many have been found in the area from Arkansas to Ohio that they must have been used for something.

Possibly some of the problematical objects in our museum collections were worn as ornaments. The plummet stones, which are also known as plumb bobs and net weights, were shaped liked the plummet weights carpenters use today. Discoidals, or flat, round, carefully worked disks of stone may have served a variety of uses. Some are slightly concave and show traces of color on their surfaces, as if they had been used

"Problematic objects" include bird-stones and butterfly-stones

as palettes for mixing paints. Others, perhaps, were used as throwing stones in games—we have a description of an early-day Creek game called "chunky," in which such stones were used like quoits. And just possibly some of the discoidals or the plummet-shaped or boat-shaped stones were used in polishing pottery. Certainly stones of some kind were used to rub the surfaces of vessels to produce the high luster we still see on many of them.

When only one or two examples of a given type of artifact are found in a series of excavations, archaeologists sometimes assume that these artifacts were intended for use in ceremonies.

But when there are a great many identical or similar specimens of a type artifact scattered over a wide area, it is usual to decide that they must have been utility articles, whether we moderns have been able to determine their exact use or not. This probably is the case with many of the specimens we have just described as problematical objects. Some day the use will be determined, and everyone will be surprised that it was not discovered long ago.

But to return to President Jefferson and his writing and correspondence. The president suggested that the mounds were "incalculably old," as well as that they must have been constructed by the members of a "vanished race." In making this suggestion he was not allowing for the events of history; after all, what is history to us today was current events to Thomas Jefferson.

For instance, as soon as the white men overran part of the continent and conquered the Indians who lived there, the Indians changed most of their habits. From having been free and independent souls, dealing with all other men as equals, they became first the prisoners of war and later the wards of the conquerors. Like all oppressed people everywhere they were unhappy. They had lost their freedom, they were desperately poor, and they had little or no incentive to improve their condition.

When people are hungry all the time; when they have been deprived of their only way of earning a living; when they can see nothing ahead for themselves and their children but disease, poverty, and despair, they are too tired and discouraged to think about building mounds, or carving pipes, or indeed doing much of anything. So it came about that many of the Eastern Indians appeared to the white men of President Jefferson's day as being "incapable of constructing monumental mounds and earthworks." The Indians had no incentive and no strength left for doing that kind of work.

In the last century and a half, we have learned more and more about the Indians who did build the mounds. We have not yet come to the end of things to be learned about these people, and it is too soon to guess when we will run out of new facts. Every new scientific method that is developed in any field is tested to see whether it can be applied to archaeology.

Aerial photography, for instance, has made possible some dramatic new archaeological discoveries. This method of mapping is particularly important as a means of locating new sites, such as low mounds, for shadows and shapes will often be clearly apparent from the air although they may be invisible at ground level.

Of course, even when a site has been located from the air and explored on the ground, we still don't necessarily know how old it is. In many cases its age may still be "incalculable." If the site is postwhite, and trade goods are included among the Indian artifacts it contains, the matter is easier. If a piece of chain, or a gunlock, or a string of glass beads, or a knife, or half a pair of scissors turns up in the undisturbed earth, then we can safely say that the mound was built after history began. This is especially the case when the trade goods are found in direct association with artifacts made by the Indians. Then we know that the artifacts, too, are probably postwhite, and we can begin the long and laborious process of cross-dating them. From the minimum date of the first white trading in the area, we can go on to maximum dates of manufacture.

But when everything that is found in a site is indubitably Indian, and when all the artifacts appear to have been made at the same time and to have been buried together, it is much harder to determine how old any of the artifacts in the site may be. About all we can say safely is that they are prewhite, that they were made in prehistoric times. In such a case, the best we can do is hope that a trade piece will appear. Next best is an artifact similar to those excavated from a postwhite site.

Long before the white men landed, the Indians traded goods with one another. Sometimes there is no overlap in time; sometimes there is. Then an artifact from a dated site may be found in a previously undated one. In that way, we can *estimate* the age of the undated site. It cannot be *older* than the dated artifact, but it *can* be younger. Cross-dating is very useful as a tool for gauging times and dates, but unfortunately it is not always possible.

Another method of dating, still being worked out, is by means of fossil pollens. It works better in the northern regions than in southern ones, and it was first developed in Scandinavia.

This method is based on geological information. As the glaciers of the ice ages moved forward, there was naturally a change in the varieties of vegetation everywhere. Some kinds of plant life died out, others thrived. Then—presumably because the earth had tipped slightly and exposed another part of its surface to the sun as a result of the weight of the ice or because the weight of the ice caused the earth's surface beneath it to slip—the glaciers melted and withdrew, and again the vegetation changed. Plant life began to spread northward.

Often a glaciated area is clearly marked, for geologists, by a layer of smoothly rounded, gravellike pebbles. The stones were ground down, smoothed, polished, pushed forward, and finally deposited by the advance and retreat of the icecap. Above and below the glaciation level, plant pollens usually can be found in the subsoil. At the deepest levels will be found pollens of tropical or subtropical plants; above them the pollens of plants of the temperate zones can be identified; and at the top, nearest the glacier's surface, will be found subarctic and arctic plants of tundra growth.

The buried—or fossil—pollens do not furnish the archae-ologists with an absolute method of dating, but they do supply a comparative one. Fossil pollens can give an idea of how long ago, in relation to the last ice age, certain sites were built and occupied.

Another dating method—one that can be used anywhere, in once-glaciated terrain or in unglaciated terrain—is the use of Carbon 14. This method is based on one of the discoveries made in the field of atomic physics, which shows again how scientific fields can interlock.

All living organisms—plants and animals of all sorts—take in carbon and give it off again at a constant rate, so that a balance of carbon content is maintained by the organism. After the plant or animal dies, it continues to give off carbon at the same known rate, but without taking any in. The balance is disturbed, and the amount of residual carbon in the organism steadily decreases.

The amount of carbon given off by organic, or once-living, materials has been proved to depend on the age of the material. That is, Carbon 14 dating can be used to determine how long ago a tree was cut down to make a beam, or when an armful of rushes was gathered to make a mat. The method is useless in dating stone artifacts, which never were alive, and it is almost useless in dating pottery sherds because the amounts of shell or vegetable matter that may have been used to temper the clay are too small in relation to the clay mass to mean anything.

Carbon 14 dating has not yet been perfected to the point where it can be used with pinpoint accuracy. There is still a margin of error; a piece may be older or younger than its Carbon 14 date. It varies from $\pm$ 50 years to $\pm$ 5,000 or more. As time goes on and more specimens are tested, the margin of error will naturally be reduced. So far, the oldest known Carbon 14 date is 43,000 years ago.

Physicists and archaeologists are working together to reduce the margin of error. Even ± 400 years, which has been given in many archaeological publications, is a lot of margin when we are dealing with human beings and their cultures. Four hundred years ago, white men had barely set foot in North America. Look at what has happened to this continent since 1559! Even fifty years has brought considerable amounts of change in human life; in the opening paragraph of this book we spoke of what life would be like if everything before 1900 could be canceled out. However, fifty years is a workable period, and archaeologists will probably be satisfied to work within this framework.

So here we must fall back, again, on comparative information. We must rely on data that geologists and physicists are able to furnish for the use of archaeologists and historians. There must be continual, endless checking and cross-checking of the data of one science against those of another. Even skeletons and dessicated mummies can be used in dating. Sometimes those found in North American sites show traces of disease that is known to be of New World origin; sometimes they reveal that the person died of an Old World illness like tuberculosis. In the last years of Indian time—the protohistoric period—many of the white men's sicknesses, such as smallpox, measles, chickenpox, and common colds reached Indian tribes the white men had not yet visited, and killed thousands of people in the first great epidemics to sweep across the continent. However, these diseases, unlike tuberculosis, do not leave traces of their passage on the skeleton.

Carbon 14 dating perhaps could be perfected and made more accurate by means of more specimens with known dates. These can be pieces of wood from old houses that are being torn down, for instance, if you can find out in what year a certain house was built. Often cities keep permanent records of building permits that have been issued. You can find out how old a house is by consulting the records at the City Hall.

Or a Carbon 14 sample can be a piece of wood or upholstery fabric from an old piece of furniture—again, if you can find out when the table or chair or sofa in question was made. (Be sure that it is something that has been discarded as unusable; *don't* go around cutting samples out of people's antiques.) While your local museum director may not have the expensive and elaborate material that will be needed to test the sample, he will know who does. Then the specimen can be sent away for testing, and its Carbon 14 content can be permanently recorded.

There are many things that hobby archaeologists, even beginners, can do to help the professionals. Their help is especially valuable in parts of the country that are already densely settled, or where communities are spreading out rapidly. You might even be able to find a mound yourself, by making a surface survey.

This will mean walking, particularly along riverbanks. It

will mean walking slowly and looking all around you—using all your powers of observation. The best time of year for mound-hunting is late fall or early spring, when the leaves are off the trees, and when other vegetation is curled and crisped underfoot. Then, without foliage to confuse you, it is possible to see the shape of the country around you.

Always remember: Never go onto somebody's property, even to look for mounds, without first getting permission from the owner or occupant of the land.

If you do find what you think is a mound (although it *could* be a small natural hill), try walking around its base. Watch the ground underfoot as you go. See if the earth is all the same color, or if there are lighter or darker streaks running outward from the base of the mound. Usually, if the mound was built up intentionally and didn't just happen, there will be differences in color—sometimes slight, sometimes considerable—showing on the earth around it. Look for them first. If you find them, you will be ready for the next step.

Start at the base of the mound and work out from it in as nearly a straight line as you can, going downhill if possible. This time you are looking for potsherds (little fragments of broken pottery) and bits of worked stone. Remember, at the same time, that purposely chipped stone and naturally broken stone look about the same to an untrained eye, and have even been known to confuse the experts.

Watch the ground before you closely. Examine every piece

of stone that you find. Sometimes pottery that has lain on the surface of the ground, exposed to weather, looks more like stone than anything else. If you find potsherds, or stone samples that you feel reasonably sure are artifacts, put your specimens in a paper bag, and write on the bag precisely when and where you found them. You can do this exploring best after a heavy rain or a high wind, when the natural forces have disturbed the surface of the ground and brought new artifacts to light.

Always take a compass with you, and a measuring tape, and some lunch. Try to determine whether the mound slopes more in one direction than another, and what the compass bearing of the sloping side is. You may only confirm previous information about the direction of the prevailing winds in the area. On the other hand, you may have gained a small piece of information about the how and the why of the building of the mound.

Make notes of all your observations in some kind of small field notebook. If you have a camera, take it along on your expedition; the more pictures you take of possible sites, the better. They probably won't be very exciting to look at, as pictures go. But they may quite possibly be clear enough to tell an archaeologist whether what you have found is a mound or a natural hill.

If all this sounds like a lot of work, it is. It is necessary work. Somebody has to do it before any other work can begin. In one sense, this is all routine work, but it carries with it the excitement of discovery. And an untrained as well as a trained worker can do it, thus freeing the archaeologist for more advanced work that only he can do. If you can learn to make preliminary surveys, you will be on your way to making other contributions to the science of archaeology.

Above everything else, unless you have a state license *and* an expert along to supervise you, *don't dig*. Learn to use your powers of observation to the point where you can rely on them.

The more pictures taken of possible sites, the better

They are probably much better than you think. Those of us who make a habit of living with television and air conditioning don't use half the faculties we were born with. In field archaeology nothing takes the place of *your* care in watching and working, *your* respect for the past, and *your* readiness to think for yourself and then cooperate with other people.

You must learn first of all to be content with accomplishing as much as you can on the surface of the ground, without disturbing anything that lies beneath it. Leave your spades and trowels at home. They're heavy and awkward to carry around, at the best. What you can pick up with your own fingers, or scratch from the earth with a pocketknife, is the kind of specimen you are looking for in a surface survey.

When you have made your pictures and notes and gathered your surface specimens, you are ready to report your find. Now your local museum director is truly your best friend. Take or send everything you have found, together with prints of your photographs and copies of your field notes, to him. Make a very brief report of where you went, why you decided to go there, what you found, and what you observed that might lead to further discoveries. Then, and only then, you may ask the director if, when he has time and opportunity to visit your site, you may go with him. He will probably be glad to have you save him time by taking him to the spot.

The first time you watch an expert archaeologist in action in the field, you will probably be disappointed. He won't appear to be doing much more than you have already done yourself. He may cover more ground in less time than you did. You showed him where to go in the first place. In the second, he has training and experience you lack, or your roles would be reversed. All the same, the archaeologist's first surface survey or superficial examination will be very much the same as the one you made. He is concerned, first of all, with confirming your find so it can be entered on the master map which records all discoveries in your area.

And you will probably decide before the first day is over that your expert spends an awful lot of his time talking. Naturally, he will want to talk to the owner or tenant of the land before he starts for the site. In the first place, he has to get permission to go on the property, just as you did, so he will not be accused of trespassing. In the second place, he wants to know whatever the man who lives there can tell him about the site. Perhaps the farmer has potsherds, or stone blades or points, or even large, intact artifacts, that he has plowed or dug up near the mound. Perhaps he may know of other, similar sites near by that you have not located. The archaeologist acquires as much as he can of this information. Listening is a useful tool.

Even after you have made a find and an archaeologist has confirmed it, even after it has been entered on the master map, it may be years before anybody starts digging at the site. If a farmer objects to having his property excavated by university or museum personnel as well as by amateurs, that is the end of the matter as long as that farmer is on that land.

Besides, in all parts of the country, salvage archaeology comes first. Unless there is danger that a road may be built right through the middle of that particular site, or that a dam will be constructed downstream, flooding and obliterating the site, it may be allowed to wait while salvage work is being done somewhere else.

Delay is especially likely to occur if the landowner is understanding and cooperative, contradictory as that statement sounds. If he is a man who senses the value of archaeology, and who is willing to work around a site and leave it intact when he plows or cultivates his land, that site will be left undisturbed. It may be years until time, men, and money are available for the excavation, and there is no pressure or haste about doing the work. On the other hand, uncooperative owners have been known deliberately to obliterate sites. Sometimes they have said that it is sacrilege to dig up the dead, some times that they just don't want strangers coming on their property for any reason. When permission is given reluctantly, it is a good idea to take advantage of it immediately.

Many times hobby archaeologists who have located prehistoric sites, but who have been careful not to dig in them or disturb the material around them are disappointed when no work is done for years after they have reported the site to the nearest trained archaeologist. Their feelings are hurt because they think that something of primary importance is being neglected.

If hobby archaeologists, in such situations, will stop and think for a moment about how few trained archaeologists there are in comparison to the number of sites; if they will remind themselves how slow and painstaking the work of excavating any site must be; and, above all, if they will reflect for a moment how roads and dams, highways and bridges, not to mention the outward spread of cities, are constantly changing the face of our land—then, perhaps, they will be consoled for this seeming neglect. First things must always come first, in any field. Nowadays, salvage archaeology is being given precedence over the more deliberate type of excavation.

10 *The Wide Open Spaces*

THE TROUBLE WITH DOING ARCHAEOLOGICAL WORK ON THE west side of the Cross Timbers, within the Great Plains region that lies at the heart of our continent, is that the spaces there are so wide and so open that it is hard to discover the archaeological sites that are dotted over the area. Even when the sites have been located and identified, the material that they once contained often has been scattered by man, time, and the weather. Consequently, trying to recreate the sequence of events on the Plains before the white men came there is hard work. Describing the lives of the Indians who once lived on the margins and along the streams of the wide grasslands is harder still.

We might almost risk saying that in the very earliest days

the broad stretch of country between the western edge of the Cross Timbers and the Rocky Mountains, from east to west, and between the Arctic Circle and northern Mexican desert from north to south, was unoccupied. Some excavation has been done, and some sites have been reported on, from the Oklahoma and Texas panhandles of the southern Plains. Most of the intensive archaeological studies of the Great Plains, however, have been concentrated in the basin of the Missouri River and its tributaries. These studies are not yet completed, and only a little of the information that has been uncovered has been published. So far, it seems that the word we are most likely to use in discussing the early Indian life of the Great Plains is "marginal."

Many of these Indians lived in villages of large earth lodges on the margins of the open grasslands. They lived along the banks of the rivers in similar villages. They lived on the lowest foothills of the Rocky Mountains, and they lived on the western fringes of the Cross Timbers. In this sense, their life was marginal to that of the Indians in the adjoining areas. The peoples of the marginal Plains made a little of this and a little of that in the way of crafts. In some ways they were like the Eastern tribes, while in others they resembled some of the peoples of the Southwest.

It would seem that the very means of subsistence of the earliest Plains Indians, as well as their way of existence, were what social scientists mean when they say "marginal." They were part-time farmers, raising the hemispheric American vegetable triad: corn, beans, and squashes, and a little cultivated tobacco to burn as incense in their ceremonies.

These Indians also hunted birds, small game, and deer. Sometimes, particularly in spring and fall when the buffalo hides were prime, they drove this largest of American game animals over cliffs to thud to death in the valleys below. The buffalo that survived the fall were slaughtered with clubs, spears, or bows and arrows at the foot of the bluff. These Indians certainly must have known how to dry the buffalo meat and save it from season to season, but their hunting methods were so uncertain that we wonder whether these people ever really had enough to eat.

They lived on the banks of streams and rivers, and they were often hungry. Therefore, it is not surprising that bone fishhooks have been found in some of the village sites. They have not been found in others, and many modern Plains Indians refuse to eat fish on religious grounds, so the distribution of the custom probably was always limited.

Like most other agriculturalists, the Indians who lived on the edges of the Great Plains made pottery. Most of it was crude and heavy and homely; incising and cord impressing seem to have been the only decorative methods they knew or used with any frequency. Some potsherds have been found with their edges so badly worn away that perhaps the wares were not even fired. The pieces may have been set outside to dry, first in the shade and then in the sun, and never baked at all.

Along the northern rivers, and especially in the upper Missouri basin, there are found the remains of the community houses that were the homes of the early Plains Indians, and were occupied by them even into historic times. These houses were semisubterranean (half underground), and each one must have sheltered several families. The structures were round, with wattle-daub walls above the ground, and roofs made of poles and brush. To enter or leave the house, the occupants climbed down or up a notched pole that had been set in the floor with its upper end resting against the edge of a hole in the roof. The same opening apparently served as both doorway and chimney; the community fire was built in a hole in the floor at the foot of the ladder. In bad weather, going in or out of the house must have been a smelly, smoky, unpleasant experience.

Around the walls of the pit house were shelf beds, made by setting forked sticks in the earth floor, laying poles from end to end between their crotches, and then laying willow branches across the poles. Sagebrush and dried grass were piled above the willows, like a mattress laid over springs. Over everything else were laid buffalo hides tanned with the hair on and laid with the fur side down to make the surface more springy. These were good, comfortable beds, better than those in many other Indians' homes. In places where abandoned houses are found to have collapsed, so that their roofs fell in and wind-drifted earth gradually filled the pits that once were houses, these beds have been discovered still in place.

In the southern part of the area, the remains of a quite different type of pit house have been reported. These structures are distinguished from the northern, earth-lodge type by being called slab houses. The inner walls of the dwellings were faced with slabs of sandstone, and sometimes other thin slabs were laid over the earth to make a floor. The great difference between pit houses and slab houses seems to have resulted at least in part from the kind of country where each was built. The deep pit-house people, as we have said, lived along the streams in the northern part of the Plains. They needed their deep shelters for protection against the severe winters of the region. The earth in their territory was a sandy loam, and was not hard to dig and pack when it thawed in the spring. These Indians also lived near wooded areas where the trees grew tall, so they had access to large logs which could be used for ceiling beams, or for uprights to support the beams and shore up the earth walls.

But in the southern Plains the soil was much sandier than in the north. While it is no problem to dig a hole in sandy soil even without metal shovels, making the hole stay dug is another matter. That probably was the reason the southern Indians used sandstone slabs to support their interior walls. A flat surface would hold back the sliding earth, and prevent the house from falling in on its occupants. Slab houses seem to have been single-family dwellings, set in clustered groups. They certainly never were as large as the northern pit houses. After all, the people of the southern Plains lived in an almost woodless area. About all they could count on for poles and beams were mesquite and creosote bushes, which weren't big enough to do anybody any good; or cottonwoods, which break easily under any weight.

However, it is in the dry climate of the southern Plains that archaeologists have been able to make some progress with what is called "maximum cross-dating." In one of the slab houses excavated near Optima, in the Oklahoma panhandle, some good hard potsherds were discovered. They were decorated with designs of fine black lines painted on a polished white surface.

Although these sherds had been found in a southern Plains site, they were not in the least like the heavy, unpainted wares that had been turned up elsewhere on the Plains. The Optima sherds looked for all the world like the pottery made by Indians who lived in the stone apartment-house villages (we call the cities by their Spanish name for towns—pueblos) of prehistoric New Mexico and Arizona, Utah and Colorado.

Here was a problem in cross-dating. The sherds from the Optima slab house were sent to the Laboratory of Anthropology at Sante Fe, New Mexico. There the fragments were examined by experts on the pottery of the prehistoric Southwest, and finally a date was assigned to the handful of sherds. It was decided that the original vessel from which they came had been made in New Mexico during the Pueblo III period, probably about our year 1100. The A.D. 1100 date meant that the Optima site *could* be as much as eight hundred years old. It could also be as little as two hundred years old. The age of the site depended on the time when the vessel was dropped and abandoned by its owner, perhaps in the course of moving to another home. If the Optima people communicated directly with the people who lived near Santa Fe in the Pueblo III period, perhaps trading salt to them and getting pottery in return, then the eight-hundred-year-old date was possible.

But if what had happened was that someone from proto-historic or even historic Optima, on a visit or an Indian business trip to New Mexico, had just happened to pick up some pretty painted sherds he found scattered around, and bring them home for his children to play with, then the Optima site could be much less than the eight hundred year maximum. Similar sherds have been found in the Texas panhandle since the Optima discovery was made, and it seems probable that the date of pottery-making was contemporary with the date of slab-house occupancy. However, that is only on the basis of what we know *now,* and the matter is still far from settled. Many of the most important discoveries in the Texas panhandle, by the way, have been made by amateur, or hobby, archaeologists in the course of surface surveys.

Fortunately for everybody concerned, particularly the archaeologists, the Optima sherds matched each other closely enough to show that a whole vessel had been brought from New Mexico, and later had been broken. That was enough to assign a probable prehistoric date to the site.

Cross-dating like this is one of the most fascinating parts of playing the archaeology game. It is as risky as chess, because the unknown factors are numerous—so numerous that often the players can only guess what they *might* be. Always remember that *ideas* travel from one group of people to another as readily as *objects* do. Also, remember that whether it is an idea or an artifact that is being transported, it will need time to travel, and to pass from one group to another. If it took the first American settlers twenty thousand years to occupy the continent, eight hundred years seems like a brief time indeed by comparison. Every cross-dating problem bears a red *danger* label. Archaeologists are extremely cautious about relying on that method by itself.

The Great Plains area is enormous—a third of the continent. We might say that, while it is thoroughly populated, it has never been entirely explored. New sites are discovered there every year, and nobody can guess how many more are still waiting to be found. More than any other part of the United States and Canada, the Plains area still waits to be learned by walking. And it is so big and wide and open that the mere thought of walking over it is enough to discourage everybody, as it seems to have discouraged the early Indians.

The prehistoric plainsmen generally stuck to their safe marginal areas. Only small, straggling hunting-exploring parties set out onto the vast land-ocean of the Plains—as far as we know now.

Our first written description of the Plains area comes from the report of Francisco Vasquez de Coronado. The document was made on his return from his expedition northward from Mexico City, a trip that he began in 1540 and ended three years later. The village Indians of the Southwest, this Spanish soldier wrote, sent him journeying northeastward (he said they sent him "mas alla"—"further on") into the grasslands. He had originally started out to discover what were called then the Seven Cities of Cíbola ("cíbola" is the Spanish word for buffalo), and the Indians of southern New Mexico assured him that he would find the cities somewhere in the area that is southwest Kansas or northwestern Oklahoma now. Coronado did not find the seven famous cities, only "mean and poor" villages, but he did find plenty of "cíbola."

Sometimes I wonder if the Southwestern Indians, who may have picked up a little Spanish by Coronado's time, weren't playing a joke on him. They could have sent him out to look for "cíbola," without being specific about the cities he thought they were referring to. Most Indians I have known and worked with in the Southwest enjoyed puns, and were good at making them. This could have been an Indian joke—but, if it were, Coronado seems to have missed the point. Like a good many other uninformed persons, he may have thought the Indians had no sense of humor.

Coronado not only didn't find the cities, he lost some of his horses. He and his men straggled back to the Rio Grande. They spent what was left of a bleak winter with the Indians of the city of Tiguex (Tee-wesh), not far north of the place where the city of Albuquerque sprawls today. The walled ruins of Tiguex are still standing, and are a state monument now. Here the Spaniards rested from their struggle with the grasses that grew taller than men's heads from the soil of the Plains. Here the Spaniards may have tried to forget about the great "cattle" that lived on the grasslands, and were only too ready to come charging through the dense growth to attack any men or other moving objects that disturbed them.

We'll come back to Coronado later on. He and his followers —and with them the other Spaniards who came in later bands —fulfilled their purpose, as far as the Plains Indians were concerned, by losing those horses.

At first sight the Indians—from Mexico north—had thought that horse and man were a single miraculous beast, one that was able to split itself in two when it was attacked by an enemy. But the Indians soon learned that the upper, detachable halves of these centaurs were men, and that they were really no stronger or more dangerous than other men, once they were on foot. It was the horses that had greater strength and endurance than the only domesticated animals the Indians had ever known. It was the horses that carried heavy men and heavier armor over great distances in rough country. Horses were the Spaniards' secret weapons, and the source of their superiority in fighting with the Indians. And horses, as the Indians presently learned, could be stolen at night from the Spanish camps. Once the Indians obtained the horses they would be potentially equal to the Spaniards in mobility and in fighting. Better, because they knew more about the country.

Now it was as if a door had been opened to the people. The Indians poured out of their dark underground houses into the free world of the sunlight. They retained little from their old way of life, for there were few parts of it as important to them as movement and the freedom to move. Certainly they remembered nothing from their collective past that seemed as important as the knowledge they gained of their new present. Tribes from the north, the east, and the west of the Plains met each other. Their beliefs and customs mingled, and a single way of life came into being for all of them. How far to the south the Plains way of life spread is still undetermined. There is little doubt about how far it might have gone if other white men and their weapons had not come into the picture.

As soon as the people left their holes in the ground, and began to live on the earth's sunny surface, they needed a new type of shelter. Perhaps they already knew about the conical skin tents we call by their Dakota Siouan name "tipis." Perhaps hunters had used small tipis in the past. Now the tipi became the only shelter used by the Plains Indians, and they used it the year round. Tipis were large or small, painted or

Painted tipis made of buffalo hides

undecorated; they had as few as twelve supporting poles or as many as twenty-four, but they were always portable.

When the women of the marginal Plains became the women of the true Plains, they gave up making pottery and baskets in favor of making containers and vessels of buffalo hide. Soon only the children kept alive the memory of the older skills by teaching one another how to make toys. They turned out clumsy little bowls and oddly shaped clay figurines; they coiled and sewed grasses together to make play baskets. The women were all too busy making bags and boxes and envelopes and tubular cases of rawhide or dressed skins to be bothered with heavier, more laborious work. The mothers wanted only things that were light in weight and easy to carry around with them on horseback.

And the mothers no longer took care of their babies in the old-fashioned ways. Instead of putting the little children into hammock cradles, hung from the house rafters or from pole frames outdoors, the mothers made carrying cases that could be slung from their saddle horns or between their shoulders, or set on the ground leaning against the tipi wall. The children actually were safer and more protected in the carrying cradles (which are sometimes called cradleboards, or baby boards, or even, unfortunately, papoose boards, and which have no *one* name) than they had been in the hammocks. The big horseback cradles, babies and all, were easily carried around whenever a village moved its camp. No family need be left behind by the others because it had a small baby to care for.

So here we are, at the outside edge of prehistory again. These events took place in the period of protohistory of the Plains area. That is, the fifty or seventy-five or, at most, one hundred years before the Louisiana Purchase of 1802, and the Lewis and Clark Expedition that followed in 1803. The great horseback change in Plains Indian life must have taken place a comparatively short time before those two events ended the prehistoric period on the Plains. As soon as Lewis and Clark returned from their trip and wrote down their report to President Jefferson, Plains prehistory was over.

Of course the ending of prehistory was not the end of the Plains Indians, only the beginning of a new phase in their history of themselves. The descendants of the original tribes still live in parts of the Plains area and still think of it as their home. But the Plains Indians of today are generally peaceful farmers and businessmen. They do not look in the least like the flashing, brilliant, daring warriors whom the whites finally subdued in the 1870's. Nowadays, except at their social and religious dances, the Plains Indians look much like all the rest of us.

Most Indians, wherever they lived, had tribal names for themselves. Nearly always these names, when they are translated, mean "people," or "men." The Plains Indians must have been men indeed, for most of us, when we hear the word "Indian," automatically think of war-bonneted horseback figures, glinting and alive in the sun, in color and motion. The Plains Indians represented all Indians for most of us.

11 *Archaeology on the Hoof*

IN THE AMERICAN SOUTHWEST, FROM THE MOUNTAINS OF SOUTH-
ern Utah and Colorado to the deserts of northern Mexico, there
was once a dense Indian population. Portions of that area are
still occupied by their descendants, although most of it was
long ago overrun by white men. Along the Rio Grande drainage and the desert uplands of Arizona we find today groups
of Indians who have strong religious reasons for preserving the
customs and faith of their ancestors.

These are the Indians whom we know by the Spanish phrase
Pueblo (or village) Indians. They include the people of the
Rio Grande villages, those west of them in the towns of Laguna
and Acoma, and those still west again at Zuñi and the Hopi
mesas.

Once upon a time all these Indian communities and more,

with the fertile fields that surrounded them, extended from the Mesa Verde (the Green Tableland) in Colorado to the Casas Grandes (the Great Houses) of the Mexican state of Chihuahua. As time goes on, and archaeological work is extended over an ever-widening area, we find that the Pueblo territory is also being extended. More and more of the arid lands of the Southwest prove to have been the former homelands of a settled, prosperous, agricultural, artistic, and religious people.

We often use a Navaho Indian word "Anasazi" when we speak of the prehistoric Indians of this part of the Southwest. "Anasazi" means "The People Who Went Before," and they and their descendants are the people we are talking about now. Although we know exactly when prehistory ended in their part of the Southwest—it was in 1540, when Coronado and his followers arrived—it is still possible to describe many aspects of the lives of the Anasazi by describing the lives of their living descendants. In some ways, this life was very little changed by the white invasion.

Fortunately for archaeology, almost all the sites that are identified with the Anasazi were located in places where the climate was and is extremely dry. For that reason many substances, such as the fibers used in making baskets, mats, and fabrics, have not rotted away with time. They have simply dried up. Their colors have faded and blurred a little, but many of the artifacts have remained where they were, looking as they did when their owners buried them.

Today we see archaeology on the hoof in the Southwestern Indian villages

So, for that matter, have the owners themselves, not to mention their pet dogs. We often read or hear of "mummies" that have been taken from Southwestern sites, particularly from those in caves or bluff shelters. These are not the true mummies—with their body cavities emptied of organs and refilled with spices and herbs; with the outer parts of the bodies embalmed and swathed in scented linen bandages—that have been unearthed in Egypt. Anasazi mummies are bodies that have dried out to a leathery-crisp toughness through resting for centuries in a dry country. Men, women, and children—some of them, as we have said, with their little brown or white or spotted dogs—have been discovered. Many of the Anasazi mummies have found their later resting places in our museums.

We haven't room or time enough for a detailed description of the life of the Anasazi and their descendants in this chapter. After all, what primarily interests us in this book is archaeology as a science. We are particularly concerned with the methods modern archaeologists use in conducting their research. Because the most accurate method known so far in dating archaeological material was developed in the Southwest, dating and its methods will take up a good deal of this section of the book.

We might as well begin with the caves, and the materials that are found in them—sometimes in association with the mummies, sometimes alone. Some of the oldest evidences of human life in the Americas have been found in a cave in the Sandia Mountains, northeast of Albuquerque, New Mexico. Other famous Southwestern caves, not so old as Sandia Cave, are Bat Cave, Painted Cave, and Montezuma's Castle Cave.

Here we will have to learn a new word: stratigraphy. "Strata" are layers, and "graph" is writing. Archaeology has taken the word over from geology, where it was first used to describe the layers of rocks and soil between the core and the surface of the earth. Archaeology uses the word stratigraphy to describe the successive layers of occupancy in any site.

For instance, let us assume that we are excavating a cave. Its prehistoric occupants have left us the charcoal of their cooking fires; their worn-out and discarded mats and baskets; their broken or forgotten weapons; the scraps of food left over from their meals, and their lost or mislaid jewelry and ornaments and garments. All these things were left lying around when the cave dwellers moved on, whether the cave happens to be in the Missouri Ozarks or the New Mexico Sandias.

The significant difference between them happens to be in climate. The climate of the Ozarks is relatively moist. We have simply no way of knowing how much abandoned material rotted away before white men entered the Ozark caves, but there must have been a lot of it. In the Southwest, the climate is extremely dry. After the first occupants abandoned their cave and left it standing empty to the weather, the strong winds blew in a layer of dust—powder-fine and powder-dry—that covered up all the earliest traces of human life. Later on, other Indians moved into what they thought had always been an unoccupied cave. In their turn, the second group of tenants moved on, leaving their possessions and camp-site rubbish behind them. Again the dust penetrated the shelter, and again later people moved in on a dry, undisturbed surface. So the living and leaving of the cave continued for centuries.

And so, as time went on, the floor level of the cave rose steadily as a result of the alternate deposits of artifacts and dust. In time the cave became one big archaeological layer cake. Perhaps, once in a while a few sherds of pottery worked their way up to the surface of the cave floor, to give an exploring archaeologist a clue to what might lie hidden below.

Take out all the surface material in a stratified site, and you will find a layer of dusty, artifact-free (or sterile) earth, which marks the end of a period of occupation. Scrape away this layer, and you will come to a second layer, this one rich in the debris of prehistoric life. Take this out, mapping and charting carefully as you go, scrape away the sterile layer that lies beneath it, and you may find another artifact-rich level. You can go on this way for quite a while, alternating scraping and charting, until you reach what appears to be the true floor of the cave. Even then, what seems to be the bottom may be a layer of tamped or puddled earth above more artifacts, and not a true rock floor at all. This was the case in Sandia Cave. When what appeared to be the floor, on which Folsom points were resting, was broken through, a new level was found, containing points of a previously unreported type. They are known now as the Sandia points, and are generally considered older than the Folsom artifacts.

It sometimes happens that the last—or upper—occupants of a cave were bats. Then the archaeologists have to dispose of a thick layer of dried guano, or bat manure, before they can get down to work. Often the guano, or a layer of wind-dropped dust, will rise in stifling clouds when it is disturbed, choking and strangling the workers. Then the archaeologists must work in respirators, with miners' lamps clipped onto their hats, to excavate the site. Sometimes the ceiling of a cave is so low that the diggers must work lying flat on their stomachs, scraping the dirt away beneath and behind them like terriers trying to get a gopher out of its burrow. Cave archaeology is not a field for people who are easily discouraged, or are subject to hay fever.

Still, for the people who can and will stick it out, cave archaeology is richly rewarding. By means of cave stratigraphy, it has been possible for archaeologists to reconstruct a whole series of populations throughout the Southwest. They can tell us approximately in what order new inventions were made by the Southwesterners, or new traits were introduced into the area by outside groups.

Comparatively late in Anasazi history, in about our year A.D. 1, the Southwestern Indians gave up the idea of living on the open floors of small caves or shelters. They began building up walls inside larger caves and bluff shelters. At the earliest time, these were simple walls of dry-laid stones, without binding mortar, used to separate the floors of the caves into living and storage units. Later, free-standing walls, sometimes as much as four or five stories high, were built—still inside the cave openings.

At about the same time that they began to build apartment houses inside caves, the Anasazi men began to work the ground

Apartment 5-B, Cliff House, Mesa Verde, Colorado

outside the shelters. Agriculture in the Southwest began, as it has continued, with corn, beans, squashes, short-staple cotton, sunflowers, and tobacco. We are not sure yet whether agriculture originated in the Southwest or was brought there from the South—from Peru to Mexico and so to New Mexico and Arizona.

Wherever it came from, the Anasazi soon came to depend on their agriculture as their main source of food. They never were and never became great hunters. The buffalo area was east of the mountains that were east of most of the Anasazi. The largest game in their territory were deer. The Indians depended more on small game than large for their meat—on rabbits, gophers, prairie dogs, and pack rats, among others. Apparently most of these Indians did not eat fish, although there were fish to be caught in the streams of the high mountains.

Apparently, the Anasazi moved about somewhat in their territory, from north to south principally. The question is, why? Many Anasazi towns were seemingly abandoned when life was going smoothly for their occupants. Even when it is possible to explain the abandonment on the grounds that the fields around a town became exhausted, or that most of the occupants died, we seldom find burials near Anasazi sites. The evidences of occupancy are abundant; the evidences of abandonment are present—what became of all the people?

There are not enough bodies or bones to explain the great number of sites or the long periods during which the cities were occupied. Perhaps some, at least, of the Anasazi followed a custom many of their descendants observe to this day: When small children die, their bodies are buried under the floors of their homes. It is believed that when the child's spirit finds itself among familiar people and surroundings it will not be afraid of the great afterworld, and will soon return to its parents in the body of another child. But the bodies of children more than a year old, and those of adults, are buried secretly outside the towns, and often are hidden away among the rocks on the mountainsides. This fact might explain our finding some mummies near the deserted cities, and still not finding enough human remains to explain the great Anasazi civilization.

And if there is a mystery about Anasazi population, it is closely connected with the mystery of Anasazi agriculture. Large populations must depend on foods they raise, otherwise they cannot exist. Only small groups of hunters or fishers or gatherers can continue to occupy a region year after year after year. Otherwise the food supply is rapidly exhausted. Farmers and those fed by farmers, like most of us, can remain fixed in one place, living in one season on the food that was stored in another.

When the Anasazi stopped depending on and gathering wild seeds for food, and began to raise field crops, they did so to such an extent that they even raised sunflowers for the oil that could be extracted from the seeds. For many years archaeologists supposed that New World agriculture, especially corn-growing, had been invented more than once, and that the Southwest was one of several places where it had developed. As new information has been recorded, however, that supposition has been gradually abandoned in favor of the theory that Indian agriculture was probably developed only once and then in Mexico, Middle America, or Peru. From the original place of its invention, agriculture gradually spread, traveling as any other idea might travel.

The mystery of corn is not yet entirely solved. We are far from knowing the answers to all the questions that could be asked about New World agriculture. Corn, for instance, is almost the only food plant—and certainly the only grain—that cannot perpetuate itself without the help of man. Corn *must* be planted if it is to grow, and that means that many people, in the course of many centuries, went to a great deal of trouble to develop it and learn how to plant it at all. Archaeologists are relying heavily on botanists and nutritionists for information that may help them in solving the corn problem.

We do know that New World agriculture reached a peak of efficiency, and became able to support large sedentary, town-living populations at about the same time that agriculture in Europe reached the same point. The time of city building and city living and city independence almost coincides on the two continents. This is another mystery; something else still to be explained. At present we can only say that science and the fine arts cannot exist in and of themselves anywhere in the world. There must be a population large enough to support the few people in each group who are capable of artistic and intellectual activity, so that they may be freed from the necessity for doing other kinds of work.

We also know that at about the same time that agriculture became important to them, the Anasazi stopped using household utensils made of basketry and began making pottery. That does not mean they stopped producing baskets, of course.

There are some activities—such as gathering wild seeds, or field crops, or picking up nuts—where baskets are better in every way than pottery. The Anasazi women continued to make baskets they needed for daily use. Yet the change from fiber to earthenware vessels and containers was so sudden and so complete that some archaeologists have called the early Southwestern Indians the Basket Makers, and the later ones the Pueblo Potters, almost as if they thought of them as two separate peoples. The word Anasazi is a more convenient term, though, because it shows the close relationships among people of the different historic periods.

We need such a general word because of the differences in time scales and sequences in different parts of the Southwest. Basket-making accompanied by wild-food gathering did not end, and pottery and agriculture begin simultaneously everywhere in the Southwest. Both crafts and industries overlapped one another; one began earlier and the other continued later in various parts of the area. Each time a new site is discovered and excavated the time-discrepancies become plainer, and the differences in rates of spread and adaptation become more apparent.

So far, we have spoken only of the Anasazi, and we have left out the other prehistoric peoples of the Southwest. One reason for that is that the Anasazi and their culture are more familiar to more of us than their contemporaries in any period. For another reason, the Anasazi area is the one part of the United

States where we know with certainty, to the year, when events took place. This exactness in dating is the result of the development of dendrochronology, or tree-ring dating.

Every tree that grows, as it grows, writes its autobiography.

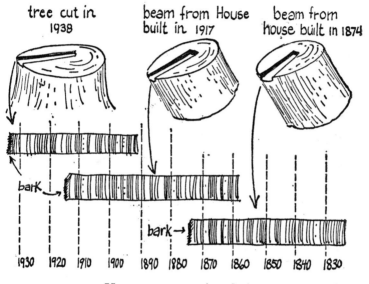

How to use tree-ring dating

It builds a ring of wood around its heart, just inside the bark, for each growing season. In a dry year the ring is narrow and dark in color; in a moist year it is wide and light in color. The most perfect diaries are those kept by the evergreens, especially the Ponderosa pines and the spruces, which grow in many parts of the Southwest. These large trees were often chosen by the Anasazi to be used as ceiling beams in their houses, or for firewood.

When a tree is cut down, you can start at its outer bark— this year's growth ring is right beneath it—and count backward until you reach the heart of the tree. Then you can figure out by subtraction in what year that tree first sprouted. You can easily see the pattern made by the successive wet and dry years during which the tree lived and continued to grow.

Then on another downed tree, you may find that, while its outer pattern is the same as that of the first, the inner section is different because it is an older tree. The two patterns overlap, and the older tree will carry your year-count farther back in time.

Later, if you can find a beam (or even a piece of charcoal) from an archaeological site and match it to the ring count you have been making, you may discover that the outer part of its growth pattern overlaps that of the inner portion of your second specimen while its inner portion, once again, is different. If you can go on matching and counting long enough—and you can find enough specimens to work with—you can figure out the growth patterns that will be common to all the trees on a given mountainside or river drainage.

This has been accomplished in our Southwest. A master chart, going back to our year 11 B.C., is available for archaeological reference. New wood samples can be compared to it, and new sites dated, quickly and easily. This is what is called dendrochronology, or tree-ring dating. It was not invented by an archaeologist, but by an astronomer, A. E. Douglass, who was interested in tracing the effect of sunspot cycles on plant growth.

In the years since Dr. Douglass developed dendrochronology, though, the method has proved as useful to archaeologists as it has been to astronomers and botanists. It is so widely used today that we sometimes almost forget that it was a contribution from another science to our own.

Naturally, there is more to dendrochronology than this too-brief explanation can tell. This is just enough to explain why those painted Pueblo III sherds found at the Optima site were so important that the experts were called on to examine and date them. If similar sherds had been dated by dendrochronology in one area, a maximum cross-date for Optima could be established. No large trees were available at Optima for comparison with beam or charcoal fragments. But as cross-dating is continued, sites east and north of Optima, containing artifacts similar to those from the Optima site, can probably be dated by this comparative method.

For the time and the area that it covers, dendrochronology is the most accurate known method of archaeological dating. It can be used as a comparison check for those elusive Carbon 14 dates. The same samples of wood can be examined equally well under the microscope and the Geiger counter. As time goes on, and scientific instruments are improved, the Carbon 14 margin of error can be reduced even more than it has been. In the Southwest dendrochronology is used as the scientific "control" for Carbon 14 calculations—the known factor by means of which the unknowns can be deduced.

Potsherd cross-dating, too, is frequently used by Southwestern archaeologists for potsherds are sometimes found in sites where no wood fragments are available. The history of Southwestern pottery types is known from dated sites, the same method being followed that was used at Optima. If the sherds show a certain decorative style, for instance, then, even though they have been excavated from sites that are distant from one another, they probably were made at the same time and place.

In a similar way it has been possible to determine when agriculture became important to the Anasazi; when basketry was largely replaced by pottery for specific uses; when the murals on the walls of ceremonial chambers (usually called by their Hopi name, kivas) were painted, and when the finest Southwestern fabrics were woven. We can trace the history of Anasazi architecture year by year, from the building of shelter walls across cave mouths to the construction of great, freestanding cities of apartment houses rising from open plains. We know more about the Anasazi than we do about any other prehistoric Indians, and still there is more and more to learn. No one of their communities was quite identical with any other. All the communities were basically similar. Some cities

Anasazi cities of apartment houses

have been proved, through the combined evidence of archaeology, history, and tribal traditions, to have been ancestral to others. It would seem that when a ceremonial, or religious, cycle ended, the people may have moved away from their old homes to establish new ones.

This statement brings us back to the point where this chapter began. The known factor that kept the Anasazi way of life alive until today in the Southwest was the Indians' religion. Today, in the Hopi villages, in Zuñi—largest of Southwestern

Indian towns—and in the communities that lie between the Rio Grande and the railroads and highways, near to the modern cities, we still see Anasazi ceremonies performed.

The Super Chief may go roaring by, and its passengers look from the windows of its air-conditioned cars at Indian men and women dressed in the same costumes and wearing the same body paints, that their ancestors wore a thousand and a thousand years ago. After the great drums have been returned to the hundred-years'-old kivas, the Indian family that has danced all day may settle down to watch a television program, and eat a meal of corn, beans, squashes, and venison that the housewife took from the deep freeze in her kitchen. These Indians see no reason why they should not enjoy the best of the old and new customs.

All the same, these Indians have proved over and over again, during the four hundred years that their history has paralleled ours, that if they are forced to choose between religion and a few modern conveniences, they will get along without the modern conveniences for a while.

In the old days, the Anasazi built their towns on points of rock, projecting into the river valleys, for defense against their Indian and white enemies. Modern Hopi men often go from ten to twenty-five miles each way each day, to reach their farm lands. These Indians are content to leave other people alone. They ask the same courtesy in return. In order to keep their religion, they are willing to live in country that most visitors term desert. It is because the Indians have remained the living past—walking human fossils—that we know as much about the Anasazi as we do.

The Anasazi descendants live in New Mexico and Arizona today

12 *And On, to Westward*

THE ANASAZI WERE NOT THE ONLY PEOPLE WHO LIVED IN THE Southwest in prehistoric times, as their descendants are not the only people who live in that region today. As we have said, we know more about the Anasazi than we do about the others, but that is certainly no reason for leaving out the other Southwestern Indians. A great deal of the archaeological field work in the modern Southwest is done outside the Anasazi area. Our knowledge of the other groups is steadily increasing.

In the rugged mountain country of southern New Mexico and Arizona, almost on the border between the United States and Mexico, there have been found traces of a group of artists whose life was different, in many ways, from that of the Anasazi. Because the most famous sites that have been excavated in this territory are located along the course of the Mimbres

River, we call the people who lived there the Mimbreños—a Spanish name that means "People of the Mimbres." They rose and flourished in the years between A.D. 900 and 1200.

The Mimbreños lived in villages along the rivers, and in a literal sense we can call them Pueblo—or town-living—Indians. A few families seem to have occupied the caves in the river bluffs at all periods of Mimbres history. They lived there as single families, though; no cave villages like those of Mesa Verde or El Rito de los Frijoles have been reported from the Mimbres area so far. All the towns that have been discovered up to the time of writing this book stood out in the open. Time—and the blowing, sifting dust—had disguised the village sites as natural mounds long before white men came into the region, or archaeologists attempted to identify them.

The Mimbreños hunted; they raised gardens, and they gathered certain wild seeds for food. Probably they were a peaceful, not a warlike, people. The few weapons that have been found in and near their homes are not primarily those of fighting men. There are throwing sticks to be hurled at rabbits and other small game, there are small, dartlike spears, and there are the knotted remnants of nets. There are plenty of stone knives and scrapers to be used in butchering game and dressing skins. The bones of antelope, of a few deer, and of many small game animals are found littered through the Mimbres village sites. These people undoubtedly wove textiles, but only small scraps of their fabrics have survived to our day.

Yet, in spite of the fact that the Mimbreños were few in numbers; in spite of the further fact that their history (as compared with Anasazi history) lasted only a brief time; in spite of the additional fact that their material life was a simple one lived in a warm climate so that relatively little in the way of artifacts was left to us—we still know many things about the Mimbreños that must be guessed at with other prehistoric Indians.

This is because the Mimbres people were potters. We can safely say that they were specialized potters. While they occasionally experimented with jars and cups, the Mimbreños by and large made bowls—thousands and thousands of bowls. Most of these bowls were of approximately the same size: eight inches across and three inches deep. There were larger and smaller specimens, of course, but the vast majority of Mimbres bowls are surprisingly uniform in size and shape.

After the bowls had been molded and dried, and a fine white clay "slip" (or finishing coat) had been applied to their surfaces and rubbed smooth and hard, the Mimbres people painted them. Sometimes the exterior of a bowl was painted, but usually the decoration was confined to the interior.

Now most Indian potters—and this is especially true of the Anasazi artists in the country north of the Mimbres—apply geometric or "abstract" designs to their wares. In almost all Indian art, designs of these types are used by women. Indian men, like male artists all over the world, paint life forms: animals, birds, fishes, insects, and people. Of all Indian arts, pottery is the one most closely identified as woman's art. Indian women invariably build the vessels, and almost invariably decorate them.

But either some of the Mimbres pottery-*painters* (as distinguished from pottery-*makers*) were men, or the Mimbreños were unlike all other Indians. The Mimbres bowls are covered with pictures of the life that was going on around the potters. People—and their clothing and activities—birds, animals, insects, fishes, and even plants are the most frequently used figures. Some of the human figures are so clear and vital that they must have been portraits of living people the artists knew personally.

Mimbres pottery differed from Anasazi pottery not only in its use of life forms, but in other ways. The Anasazi thought of their pottery decorations in terms of *mass;* that is, the designs covered large areas, and had a feeling of body and bulk. Anasazi designs interlock, and some of them combine fine line drawings with larger forms, but the whole idea behind their decoration seems to have been to make the surface of the static vessel appear to the eye to be in movement.

The Mimbreños, on the other hand, thought of their pottery decorations in terms of *line.* They drew, rather than painted. They seldom tried to cover all the surface of a vessel. Instead, like any other artists who emphasize line drawing, the Mimbreños realized that the space *around* their figures was as important as the figures themselves—it was what made the eye

Mimbreno potters drew lizards and hawks

observe the figure drawings. The Mimbres artists drew with a
light and steady hand, and with great observation and humor.
Most of their portraits of people are cartoons. They must have
been intended to be laughed at.

The lightness and delicacy of the Mimbres drawings, aside
from their humor, make the Mimbreños' life-form decorations
stand in a class by themselves, aside from all other Indian art.
Some vessels have been found with geometric designs drawn

on them, beautiful and intricate designs in themselves, but few and scattering compared with the Mimbres comic books.

Still another difference between Anasazi and Mimbreño art is in the use of color. Brilliantly colored earths for painting pottery were available in both areas. The Anasazi used them to a great extent, but the Mimbreños did not. Like modern draftsmen, the Southerners stuck to plain black-and-white in decorating their wares. Sometimes a Mimbres bowl is found with a dull-red design on its surface instead of the conventional black. This is the result of firing the pigment that would

. . . as well as people, on their bowls

otherwise have produced black at a temperature too low for the paint to carbonize. Sometimes this seems to have been done deliberately, to make a red-and-white bowl for a change. In other cases, the lowered firing temperature seems to have been the result of accident. There are also a few polychrome (or multicolored) Mimbres bowls, usually decorated with combinations of ochre yellows, black, and white.

And some few Mimbres bowls have been found with elaborate and intricate abstract designs, painted in mass, more like the Anasazi decorations than the other Mimbres wares. These bowls look as if the artists had been copying designs from fine blankets or baskets. Certain Mimbres bowls have been found with their inner surfaces entirely covered with narrow, concentric black-and-white lines. The different design styles have been found in all levels of the Mimbres sites, from the earliest to the latest days of their history. The marked differences in decorative styles furnish us with one more archaeological question to answer.

What *might* have happened in the Mimbres villages is the same as what has happened in recent years in some of the Rio Grande pueblos. There the women make the pottery vessels in the traditional way, using sand temper and the coil method. The women also polish and finish the surfaces of the bowls and jars. Then they turn the vessels over to the men to be painted. Sometimes a man paints life forms; sometimes he uses the style of geometric decoration we have previously associated in this chapter with women's painting. Probably a man who does that is consciously copying the work of his wife, mother, or sister. A few Pueblo Indian women paint their pottery themselves, and they always use geometric, abstract designs.

It is quite possible that the Mimbres men could have painted the pottery their women had modeled. In that case, such bowls as bear abstract designs are quite possibly the work of Mimbres women. Arguing by analogy in this way is fine intellectual fun, but it should never be confused with proof. We are still trying to solve the mysteries of the Mimbres painters, including where they came from in the first place, and where they went when they left their homes along the river.

To the west of the Mimbres area, in southwestern Arizona and northern Sonora, Mexico, archaeologists have found remains of another kind of people altogether. These are usually called the "Hohokam." Like Anasazi, this word means "Those Who Went Before," or perhaps "The Old Ancestors" would be a better translation of their Piman name. The Hohokam are believed to have been the direct ancestors of the modern Pima and Papago Indians.

The Hohokam were village-living agriculturalists, like most of the other early people of the area—especially all those we have talked about so far. Hohokam houses possibly were built in the same way as are modern Pima and Papago houses. Stalks of ocotillo—a wiry, thorny desert plant—were thrust into the ground, and lashed together with long, tough yucca leaves. Sometimes these houses were plastered over with clay, like the wattle-daub structures of the Southeast, but quite as often their sides were left open to whatever breezes there were, for this was in true desert country.

Hohokam agriculture included the inevitable triad: corn, beans, and squashes. Probably it also included tobacco and cotton, and possibly sunflowers. The fields were laid out along the rivers, and part of the moisture for growing field crops came from the annual overflow and flooding of the streams. Rich silt was deposited on the surface of the ground, and the water seeped down into the subsoil, enriching it. In the late period of their history the Hohokam improved on this agricultural method. They constructed canals, running back from the river beds, to irrigate their fields. The courses of Hohokam irrigation ditches can still be traced in air photographs.

Hohokam towns were built around central squares, which we often refer to today with the Spanish word—plazas. The plazas served as gathering places for the members of the communities. Besides the central plaza, each town had its public ball court, a space somewhat larger than one of our football fields, which was walled with earth. Around the ball ground there probably were raised seats of some kind, although some spectators certainly must have perched on the court wall. Possibly there were temples adjacent to each playing field.

Hohokam ball courts present us with yet another of the

great archaeological puzzles. They are very much like the ball courts used by the Mexican and Middle American Indians; in fact, identical courts have been found in prehistoric sites as far south as Yucatan and Guatemala. Spanish records, from their very beginning in 1520, provide us with accounts of the way the ball game was played on courts in southern and central Mexico.

The game seems to have been a combination of soccer, basketball, and jai-a-lai as shown in Tarascan pottery groups in Gilcrease Museum or Museo Nacional de Mexico; it was played with rubber balls, each one "the size of a man's two fists," and the Spaniards were more fascinated by the balls than by any other feature of the game. The conquerors immediately wrote down all that they could learn about rubber. The plant and its products were unknown in the Old World before then.

Now, exactly the same kind of rubber ball was found—dried and hardened by time, slightly shrunken in size, but otherwise intact—in a Hohokam site at Snaketown, Arizona. The natural question is: how did the ball get so far north? Can Snaketown possibly be older than the Aztec towns of central Mexico, or the Mayan towns in the Central American area? Did the game start in the north—and with what kind of ball was it first played there, since there was no rubber to be had—and travel southward from the Hohokam to the Aztecs and the Tarascans and the Zapotecs? Or was the route reversed; did the game go from south to north, and did rubber balls go with the game *idea* all the way? If the game traveled from north to south, what is a *rubber* ball doing in Arizona? When, how, and by what route did it get there? There certainly are not and never were rubber trees in that part of the New World.

This is an ideal question to be settled by dendrochronology. Unfortunately, exactly at this geographical point, dendrochronology fails us. Ocotillo is not a tree, but a bush. It forms no annual growth rings, and there are no other large plants in the Hohokam area but cacti. Large, convenient, diary-keeping trees do not grow in deserts. We face many locked doors in this country of the southwestern United States, and in the northern Mexican desert south of it. Perhaps Carbon 14, in time, will provide the keys we still need to open them.

Meantime, the slow, patient work of cross-dating southern and northern cultures continues. A great deal of comparative work has been done to relate Anasazi time sequences with those to the south of them. Since Anasazi dates can be and have been accurately determined by dendrochronology already, this is another example of the care that is taken to check one method of excavation or examination by another. It is another example, too, of why it is not a good idea to play around with excavation without professional guidance.

Careful excavation in the Hohokam area still continues, of course. The methods employed in digging out these desert towns are similar to those we described in speaking of the Spiro excavation. Of course, all methods must be modified in the field; you cannot excavate a site in the Arizona desert in precisely the same way that you do one in an eastern Oklahoma swamp.

Every smallest bit of man-worked material is hoarded and studied. The Hohokam made jewelry and charms from mussel, clam, and olivella shells that must have been carried inland from the Pacific Ocean or the Gulf of California. They sometimes inlaid their shell carvings with turquoise and lignite they had brought from the mountains to the north of them, in the Anasazi territory. Workers fastened inlays on the shells with gum from the piñon trees that grew northeastward of the Hohokam homeland.

If people traveled so far in one direction to find raw materials for their ornaments, why shouldn't they have gone equally far in another direction? Quite possibly the Hohokam traders journeyed down into Mexico. In that case, they could have brought back not only jewelry but the *idea* of the ball game, its rules and regulations; the way to build ball courts; even, in some cases, rubber balls to play it with.

Before we leave the Hohokam, we should mention their pottery. This was made by a somewhat different method than the one we have described previously. The Hohokam potters used what is called the paddle-and-anvil method of making their vessels.

The base and walls of a piece of pottery were formed by the coil method, as was all other Indian pottery. But after the walls had been built up to the desired height, they were not shaped, smoothed, and thinned with a thin shell or stone. Instead, the potter held a smooth rounded stone against the inner surface of the vessel. This was the anvil. Then she struck the place on the outside where the anvil rested against the inside with a flattened wooden paddle. She turned the vessel steadily, paddling the clay against the anvil until she had the vessel shaped as she wanted it. The walls of paddled vessels are somewhat thicker than the walls of scraped wares, and the blows of the paddle naturally give them a different texture and finish.

Hohokam pottery usually has a buff-colored background, decorated in red. A few specimens are known on which the designs appear in brown on the buff, but, as in the case of the Mimbres red-on-white wares, this may be due to intentional differences in firing. It could also be due to use of a different pigment.

Like the Mimbreños, the Hohokam painted life forms on their pottery, including birds and animals with people, in their small, all-over designs. The figures are tiny and closely set, so that a design may at first look almost like a textile, but it can usually be shown to be composed entirely of life forms. Again we have the question: Did the Hohokam women shape the vessels, and then give them to their men to paint?

In a way, the Hohokam sites remind us of Spiro. Here again we have communities that were probably more important as ceremonial centers than as towns in our sense of the word. Here again are Indians who gathered together many raw materials, assembling them from a wide area, and turned them into wealth. It was certainly wealth in the Indian sense: wealth in beauty and in skillful workmanship, if not in our sense of intrinsic values. And here, as at Spiro, there are links to the life of the Indians of Mexico—and a great geographic gap between the two groups is waiting to be filled by archaeologists. The desert country of northern Mexico stretches high and wide and far. Much of it is mountainous. All the same, men have lived in it and traveled over it, from the earliest human times on this continent. And now men must travel it again, searching for the treasures of knowledge that may be hidden somewhere in its vastness.

Now it is time to backtrack again. Several times in this book we have spoken of the living Indian descendants of prehistoric peoples. In some cases we have been able to trace the relationship between ancient and modern peoples clearly and without difficulty. Do you still remember the Earliest Ones, the peoples of the Archaic Period?

We do *not* know exactly who the living descendants of the Archaic peoples are, and we cannot identify them precisely with any living Indians. Probably they include all living Indians. There are some modern tribes whose lives at the time they first met the white men give us clues to the ways the Archaic peoples lived, however. The most striking single

In California stone carvings took the form of fish and bowls

group is probably the members of the Athabascan linguistic stock. These include several varieties of Apaches, and the Navaho.

The Athabascan peoples of the Southwest were raiders—land pirates, we might say—who came charging down out of the Northwest about our year 1200. They were primarily hunters. After they reached the Southwest, some Athabascan groups learned to plant a little corn, but the majority of them continued to rely on wild plants for such vegetable foods as they ate.

These raiders appeared on the scene armed with spears and with bows and arrows. They were efficient fighting men, as daring as the Plains Indians would prove to be in later years. The Athabascans overran the Southwest, and often

they captured the towns of the more peaceful Indians. They
did not live in the towns after they had conquered them, but
they did appropriate food and captives. Slavery was well organized among these raiders.

The Athabascan women made utility baskets for cooking
and storage, including pitch-coated wicker bottles to carry
as canteens on trips across the desert country. The women
also made a little pottery. The ware is easily recognized when
it is found in an archaeological site, for it was unlike any
other ware produced in the Southwest. This pottery was thick
and heavy; it was tempered with grit and with vegetable fibers
instead of with the fine-grained sand used by the Anasazi
and Hohokam craftswomen. When it had been fired, Athabascan pottery was a dull gray-brown in color. Usually the ware
was undecorated except, perhaps, for a twist of clay (what
is known as a filet) applied below the rim of the vessel. The
most distinctive characteristic of Athabascan pottery was a
pointed bottom, instead of a flat base. The cone shape was
developed so that a vessel could be set in a hole scraped in
the ground, and a campfire could be built up around it.
Apache and Navaho priests use just such pottery vessels today
as water drums in some of their ceremonials.

The Athabascans apparently didn't learn anything about
pottery from their Anasazi captives, but they did learn a lot
about weaving. Prehistoric Southwestern fabrics usually were
made of cotton, yucca, or sotol fibers, or of dog or mountain-

sheep hair, spun on the thigh to make strings. The earliest known example of Navaho weaving must be postwhite, for it is made of yarn spun from the wool of domestic sheep, which the Spaniards had introduced to the Southwest. This early specimen is a simple striped blanket, woven about 1700. It looks much like the woolen blankets both the Anasazi descendants and the Spanish colonial pioneers were weaving at the same period. The Anasazi weavers were men, and there is still a great deal of discussion as to why the Navaho women became the weavers among their people.

All the Athabascans learned a little about agriculture after they invaded the Southwest, although they never came to depend on this source of food supply as the Anasazi and the Hohokam did. Like the Plains tribes, the Athabascans captured (or, less politely, stole) horses from the Spaniards. In time they became famous as horse breeders and horsemen.

In the Great Basin-Plateau area, northwest of the Anasazi and their Athabascan invaders, we come to another hole in the map. People lived there, but we know very little about them yet. Archaeological work is in progress in the area. Eventually fuller information will be available to all of us. But, for the present, there is little we can say of that deadly country except that it demands determination and fortitude of the archaeologists who attempt to work there.

But beyond the Sierra Nevada range, the country changes abruptly, especially along the coast, from warm and dry to cold and wet. Archaeologically, it is most convenient for us to divide the coastal area into three main sections: northern, central, and southern.

Most of the work of the prehistoric northern coastal Indians was done in wood and other plant materials, or in bone. These people made baskets; they twisted mats and garments from the strands of yucca, willow bark, cedar bark, and other materials. We have pieces of these fabrics, and we have the reports of the Spanish missionaries in the south, and the Russian explorers in the north, to tell us that the Indians of all parts of the coast were great craftsmen. The earliest of these reports date from the late 1600's and the early 1700's.

We know that the prehistoric Indians must have had great dexterity, too, because a few samples of their work in bone, shell, and stone have survived for us to see. In the southern part of the area, particularly on the islands off the Southern California coast, the people carved vessels and figurines from soapstone. Some of these sculptures were inlaid with white shell beads set in asphalt that had been taken from the open deposits that are still found in the Los Angeles area, the La Brea pits.

Similarly, on the northern part of the Pacific Coast, particularly in coastal Washington and Vancouver Island, sculpture was a great art. From the few specimens of stone carving that have been preserved for us, we know that these Indians carved in slate and limestone. They produced figurines and small totem poles in much the same styles that their modern descendants use. We can theorize that these Indians did much of their work in wood, too, as did the Indians of historic times. Because

Stone carving was the great art of the Northwest

of the damp climate, probably, most of the wood carving has disappeared, and we can only theorize.

We can almost say that salvage archaeology got its start in the Northwest. At the time when the great dams along the Columbia River were being planned and constructed, in the early 1930's, archaeological teams combed the areas to be flooded, in order to make sure that as much information as could be was preserved. It is thanks to their foresight that we know as much as we do about the Indians who lived between the western slopes of the mountains and the Pacific Coast.

Particularly we should mention the large collection of pictographs that was salvaged in the area by means of both painting and photography. The copies of the rock pictures are still being studied. We do not yet know everything they have to tell us, but a few of the available facts can be set down now.

Before we start, though, I should make clear that the Pacific Coast is *not* the only part of North America where pictographs are found. Indeed, it would be safe to say that everywhere Indians have lived, or live now, there were some people who painted, drew, or scratched pictures on rocks. All they needed were rocks that were big enough to scratch on. And by the way, if the rocks have been painted, the resulting decorations usually are called pictographs (picture writings). On the other hand, if the designs have been scratched into the rock, or pecked into it with the point of another, sharpened, stone, they are called petroglyphs (stone writings).

A great many theories have been advanced from time to time to explain pictographs in general, and some of them in particular. Like the mounds, the surface decorations on natural stones have been explained as the remains of a "vanished,

*Pictographs include "doodles," besides pictures of living
birds and animals*

higher race"—higher, that is, than any modern Indians, if
one race can possibly be higher than another.

Pictographs have also been called "runic writings," left
by the Norsemen (whose symbol-writing consisted of runes) in
places where the Norsemen could not possibly have been. They
have been called "Indian sign writing," and every museum
director and archaeologist in the business is used to being
asked to "read" pictographs or petroglyphs written in "the
Indian language." He is also wearily used to saying that they
can't be read.

Undoubtedly, many of the rock pictures are just plain doo-
dling. A hunter, hiding behind a rock and waiting for a deer

or antelope to come along and provide the family dinner, scratched or drew on the rock a picture of the animal that he had on his mind. This occupied his time while he waited, and it also might let the animals know that he was thinking about them and would like to see them turn up—what we call imitative or sympathetic magic. But quite often, maybe because the game animal didn't get the idea as quickly as he had hoped, the hunter went on to draw star-crosses, moons, sun signs, tracks, houses or tipis, people—whatever he thought of. They were often all mixed in with random scratches, both straight and curved. When the game finally appeared, the hunter stopped scratching on the rocks and got down to the serious business of shooting.

In other instances, we can be certain that the magic and religious elements were uppermost—the most important subjects on the artists' minds. This is particularly true of rock pictures in hidden places: the walls of remote canyons, or the sides of table rocks. Some pictographs can be seen only when the light falls on them from a particular angle. Undoubtedly these hidden places were used as shrines. Generally they are associated with other archaeological sites, but are not adjacent to them.

Still other pictographs probably served as directional signs, or as pointers. They indicated the locations of springs, or of patches of wild food plants. And others, again, were probably property marks, showing where the Bear Clan had the right to dig wild potatoes, and warning the Water Clan people to keep off. Quite possibly some such markers showed the limits of a tribe's hunting territory, and warned strangers that they were trespassing on it.

You frequently hear it said that all pictographs are "immeasurably old." This is almost literally the case. It is almost impossible to tell by looking at a pictograph whether it was made in the last millennium, the last century, or the last week, unless it includes a drawing of a white man, a horse, a church, or something else that is the result of white intrusion. The modern Hopis—descendants of the Anasazi—make many pictographs. They also, to make the archaeologists' work harder, renew old ones. When the old pictures become blurred with erosion, the Hopi artists of today go out and scratch them deeper into the rock.

Almost anybody who wants to can collect pictographs. You need plenty of physical endurance, plenty more time, and a camera or drawing pad and pencils. Walk along rivers that have high steep stony banks, or across mesas, or explore on foot in regions where there are large single rocks that were deposited in their present places by glaciers or stream action. If you have an opportunity to examine cave walls, they were often used as painting surfaces by prehistoric peoples.

Probably a photograph is the best record of a petroglyph. You may have to use a flash attachment on your camera, or you may even have to rub chalk into the lines of the carving

Indians everywhere painted or scratched on rocks

to make it show clearly in the picture. If the carving is not too large, you might spread a piece of paper over it, and then rub the paper with a soft pencil or a stick of artist's charcoal. This is taking a rubbing—making a negative impression of the carving.

In the case of a painted pictograph, naturally, it is a bad idea to play around with the surface of the rock. Use your camera and flash attachment, or sit down and make an exact copy of the picture on your drawing pad. *Don't* try to make a rubbing, or to handle the surface in any way. You may remove the pigment forever.

Both petroglyphs and pictographs are easily destroyed. Many of them have been lost to us already through people's carelessness. It is a real contribution to scientific archaeology to record as many of them as you can find. The largest and finest collection in the country was gathered by a hobby archaeologist, who spent his vacations hunting and recording pictographs.

13 Discoveries That Make Headlines

SO FAR, WE HAVE TALKED PRINCIPALLY ABOUT THE DULL, STEADY, heavy, plodding field work and museum phase of archaeology. We have spoken of slowness in working, or of taking greatest possible care of every fragment; we have emphasized the need for accuracy in observation. We have emphasized, too, the need for caution and deliberation in performing all types of archaeological work. At times this must have had the result of making the world's biggest treasure hunt sound too routine even to be interesting.

And perhaps I have been unfair to archaeology in talking about it in that way. All the same, I thought it was necessary to do so. Archaeology *is* exciting—so exciting that anyone can easily be carried away by the thrill of hunting and finding, and forget everything else. It has been for that reason, and to prevent any further damage to any more archaeological sites, that

I have emphasized the unthrilling aspect of archaeology.

Archaeology does make headlines, more often than you might think it would. We mentioned the newspaper stories that referred to the Spiro site as the "King Tut's Tomb of the Arkansas Valley." And that was only one site, and only one of thousands of archaeological news stories.

Before we go any farther, let's get straight about what makes archaeological news. The news is in the *archaeology,* not in the *archaeologist.* Archaeologists as a group think of themselves as scientists, and they take a common scientific attitude about news stories. What they *do* is immensely important to them, and they want the news about it to reach anyone else who is interested in learning that news has been made. The majority of archaeologists, on the other hand, are not interested in personal publicity. Their names may be mentioned in connection with a site—there are no news stories that do not include people—but among themselves they put the site news first.

In recent years most archaeological news stories have been about Old World discoveries, or excavations in Middle and South America. Only a few have appeared about North American finds. There is another simple explanation for this statement.

Most of us are descendants of Old World immigrants, and the roots of our life are in the Eastern Hemisphere. Our numerals are an Arabic system, developed in Asia Minor. When our physicists and mathematicians need other symbols to express their problems, they draw on the Greek alphabet for such letters as π. Most of our alphabet was derived by the Romans from one the Greeks had derived from one that the Phoenicians claimed to have invented, although they may have borrowed the *idea* of an alphabet somewhere else.

We speak and write a language of northern European origin, which has been strongly influenced by the Greek and Latin spoken in Mediterranean countries, and which is related to the languages spoken in most of India.

We sit in chairs and eat and work at tables like those used by the Greeks and Romans and their descendants. Many of our designs, like the Greek key, or fret, that borders our bath towels and dishes, came to us from the same sources. The Paisley designs we use on shawls and dresses are of Persian origin. We use soap which has been perfected from a cleaning substance used in ancient Gaul, or France. Our trousers and slacks are patterned after ancient Gallic garments. The list is already long; it could be made so much longer that it would seem endless.

And besides all the other material things we have borrowed or brought from the Old World, we have our physical selves. The majority of us are the descendants of Europeans, or of people from Asia Minor. So when we read of great archaeological discoveries in the Old World, the accounts have a personal meaning for most of us. They concern our real—if remote—ancestors. So news about Old World archaeology—about the cave paintings of Lascaux, France, or of Altamira, Spain; the Dead Sea Scrolls that perhaps will be proved the ancestors of our New Testament; the treasures of gold and silver and gems and learning that were unearthed at Ur of the Chaldees which have served to make the characters of the Old Testament alive and real to many of us—all these things belong to our lives and our hearts without our being aware of the fact.

Discoveries made in Middle America—Mexico, Guatemala, Yucatan, Honduras, Nicaragua, for example—are news to us for quite a different reason. They are chapters in a still unsolved mystery story—the mystery of people who built great cities around even greater temples, who were as great artists and astronomers as the world has ever known, and who disappeared. How can we explain to ourselves a people who walked out of their houses and away from their religious shrines, their cities, and the fields that enfolded both? Nobody *knows* to this day why they did so. We are beginning to make some informed guesses about the matter. Each has a somewhat more solid factual foundation than the guess that preceded it, but still they are only guesses.

Besides the disappearance mystery that still remains to be unraveled, the people of Middle America left us their art treasures, which are often as valuable intrinsically as they are esthetically. Who wouldn't get excited about a tomb full of finely made gold jewelry, whether it happened to be excavated in Egypt, or in the State of Oaxaca, Mexico? It would be inhuman not to be thrilled by a necklace of carved jade beads with a massive turquoise pendant, no matter whether it came from China or from Guatemala. If the Spanish conquistadors, who, after all, had left the richest court in Europe to come to the New World, and many of whom were rich enough to finance their independent expeditions, could get excited about the treasures of Mexico and Peru, why shouldn't the rest of us feel the same way? No mystery, this time. We should, and we do.

Those same Spanish explorers, the first white men to reach the country north of Mexico, probably set us a precedent for underestimating the Indians of what are now the United States and Canada. They described the Indians of the Southwest as if they were the poor relations of the great kings and emperors of the lands to the south, and they wrote of them in belittling phrases. Perhaps unconsciously we follow their example when we fail to see the Northern Indians as particularly stimulating sources of news.

As time has passed, however, we have gained a much better perspective on the Indians of the Americas. We have learned that the great Mexican and Peruvian kings were on their way out when the Spaniards came; their governments would not have lasted much longer, even without the final impact of an invasion. The people would themselves, probably, have ended the rule of the god-kings who held them all enthralled.

And now that we have a better perspective, we can judge the Northern Indians more accurately, too. We can see that many of their governmental systems were alive and vital and stubborn. Four hundred years of conquest have not wiped them out entirely. Nowadays it is exciting—and it rates as a two-part story in a national magazine—when stone towers in northern New Mexico which have been known to whites, reported on, observed, diagramed by them since the 1870's, are finally excavated. It is news to all of us when a salvage archaeologist excavates from an old lake bed, in western Texas, the oldest human bones (a partial skull and long bones) so far found north of Mexico. It is also very much news when an archaeologist finds embedded in the bones of a woolly mammoth, buried in the arctic ice, the same kind of stone blade or point that was first unearthed near Folsom, New Mexico.

One of our most beautiful national parks, Mesa Verde in southern Colorado, is built around ruined cities. The last community was deserted about 1290, as mysteriously as any city in Middle America. Many of our national monuments all over the country have been set aside to preserve the remains of prehistoric American Indian cultures. There are Chaco Canyon and El Rito de los Frijoles; there are Moundville, Ocmulgee, Aztalan, and many more—and even more could be established if the necessary legislation were passed, for there are many more important sites than there are national monuments. Mesa Verde, by the way, is the only site to be designated a national park; that is, because it is so big and so rich that nothing else seemed appropriate.

Once a national park or monument has been established, so that we are all free to visit and enjoy it, it usually drops out of the news. The methods by which the archaeologists of the National Park Service work, and the finds they make in the course of the day's job, on the other hand, can become news.

In the same way, when Carbon 14 dating was first discovered, it was big news. Everyone was interested to learn that the same principles that are used in locating radioactive minerals could be applied to examining material from archaeological sites. "Midland Minnie," as the oldest Texas skeleton was first known, was headline news, even when "she" turned out to be a boy and not a girl. Anybody twenty thousand years old and still in fair condition deserves a headline.

The story of the Mimbres potters has a way of sneaking back into the news at intervals. Three articles on the craft were published in popular journals in 1957. That is probably because the Mimbres people, like their Middle American contemporaries, seem simply to have vanished. One year they were there, turning their food bowls into comic books, and the next they weren't—it was almost as sudden as that and as mysterious.

Archaeological *methods* can get into the news, too. For instance, students from the University of Oklahoma, joined by others from San Carlos University in Guatemala City, and working under the direction of archaeologists from the staffs of both institutions, have spent the last three summers skin-diving in Lake Atitlan, Guatemala. They have gone down with flippers, aqualungs, and all kinds of cameras and tools, as a serious part of their graduate training in archaeology. And they have surfaced with treasures from the ancient life of Guatemala, flung into the lake long ago by the Indians as offerings to their gods.

Ten years ago nobody thought seriously of lake diving

Skin-diving is a new archaeological technique

as a means of archaeological exploration in the Americas. It is true that a few magnificent pieces of jewelry had been recovered from the sacred wells near great ceremonial centers in Mexico and Yucatan. These specimens had been brought to the surface only with great effort. They had been found scattered more or less at random over the floors of natural cisterns. Systematic removal, with its accompanying mapping and charting, was out of the question then, and at that time there was no equipment available for diving in small bodies of water. Deep-sea diving apparatus could not be used in the sacred wells.

But skin-diving, which started as a necessity and became a sport, can be done in large or small bodies of water. It can be used for the systematic exploration of a sacred well, or for surveying and mapping a large lake before the removal of artifacts from its floor begins. Skin-divers first worked with archaeologists in the Mediterranean, recovering Greek treasures from Roman war galleys that were bringing loot home to the temples of the Empire. Since that time—1946—the method has spread widely.

Often a skin-diving expedition becomes headline news because of the great monetary value of the specimens recovered. Even more often the news is exciting only to archaeologists, when the artifacts brought to the lake's surface reveal the everyday life of the people who once used them, but are valueless in themselves. Cooking pots, pottery sieves, and workmen's tools are more frequently brought up than temple incense burners or ceremonial jewelry. The greatest contribution skin-divers can make to archaeology, probably, is mapping and photographing the areas where they work. They can provide all of us with the same detailed information about a lake's bottom that other archaeologists can supply about a woodland mound or a ruined pueblo.

It was news, in another way, when a few years ago an oil company invited Park Service archaeologists to accompany its construction crews as a new pipe line was built across New Mexico and Arizona. Working behind the trench digger used by a construction crew is very different from working on a carefully surveyed site, and even more different from working in a museum laboratory. But the archaeologists took part in this kind of field work as if they had never known any other, and were able to locate and identify many important sites that perhaps would not have been discovered otherwise. Each site was entered on a master map, for future excavation—with a note to the excavators-to-come to be careful not to hit the pipe line.

Still another news story appeared on front pages all over the country when a contractor, who was laying out a new subdivision in San Diego, California, noticed that one of his prospective streets ended at a large shell heap on the water front. He called in an archaeologist, who looked the shell heap over and reported that it was the garbage dump (or kitchen midden, to use the elegant phrase that goes into official reports) of a prehistoric community. As far as archaeologists generally are concerned, the really exciting part of this story is that the contractor was willing to stop the digging at the edge of the mound, and allow time and opportunity for scientific excavation of the site.

A story that is still so new that it has barely reached the newspapers is about the work of some physical anthropologists, who are working in partnership with archaeologists in some areas. It has been established that each race stock has well-defined blood group patterns that do not coincide with the grouping of other races. The patterns of the three main stocks can be subdivided so closely that it is now possible to tell that modern Navahos are physically, as well as linguistically, related to certain Mexican Indians; and that not only do all Eskimos speak the same language, they all have the same blood type.

An even more important facet of this story is that bones from archaeological sites can be ground fine in the human biologists' laboratories. Then the bone powder is mixed with distilled water, and a serum like a blood serum is extracted from the compound. This serum can be blood-typed, as can almost any body excretion. In this way it is sometimes possible to identify the ancient occupants of a site with their living descendants.

Yes indeed, American archaeology gets into the news. If

more people were more aware of the science, there would probably be more demand for these news stories. More of them would be published. We might even live to see the day when it would be NEWS in capital letters when an archaeologist, after years of slow, careful, unassuming, dull, scholarly work in a museum laboratory, was able to fit together two more pieces of the story of the New World and the men who dwelt there before 1492.

14 Can I Get a Job in Archaeology?

THAT'S A NATURAL QUESTION TO ASK ABOUT ANY SUBJECT IN which you are interested. Can I earn a living doing something I enjoy? The answer can decide what you do with your life, and how you feel about whatever you are doing. If you know in the beginning whether or not you can get a job, you will know better whether or not you want to go ahead and begin the study and training a professional archaeologist must have. If you don't see a chance of getting a job in your field of interest, you will probably want to keep archaeology a secondary interest—a hobby—in your life plan.

Well, there are archaeological jobs to be had, and the archaeologists who fill them successfully today often started out to do very different things. I can think of one who began his adult life as an antique dealer; of another who started out to be a musician; of several women who began in museum work as stenographers or file clerks; of men who were first photographers, painters, architectural draftsmen, or doctors; of two who began their academic careers as professors of philosophy; even of one whose first job was as a designer of women's hats. An archaeologist, it seems to me, can start from any known point.

Whatever their early training might have been, these men and women all had one quality in common. They were all interested in human beings. They wanted to know how people had lived in the past, how the life that is gone could be related to the life of the present. This study and interpretation of the factors of existence was more important to these people than anything else in the world.

So there is still a chance that even though you train yourself for another profession, and go on and practice it, archaeology will get you in the end. Why not? Why should you want to get away from it? There *are* jobs in the world for archaeologists. Nothing that you learn in any field is wasted in any other, if you will apply it.

As to the kinds of jobs, many archaeologists are university professors. They devote their lives to, and earn their livings by, training more archaeologists. We have all heard a lot of jokes about absent-minded professors. We carelessly apply the phrase today to anyone who holds down a university job, and never stop to think if it fits the man or not.

Professors of archaeology can't afford to be absent-minded.

They are always on the lookout for that elusive relationship between past and present that is the heart of their work, a relationship so subtle and so fine that it is easy to overlook. At the same time archaeology professors watch for students who are potentially serious archaeologists to be trained for the future. These men must have their minds on their jobs twenty-six hours a day; they never seem to think or talk about anything else.

A professor of archaeology, like a professor in any other subject, naturally expects to direct his students' field and laboratory work. He must be willing and able to take a group of people to the site where they plan to work, and keep them there. He must organize the camp, including its location, and he must plan each day's activities, including recreation periods. He must be his own morale officer, usually, keeping people of different backgrounds, dispositions, and outside interests in harmony and on pleasant working terms with each other and with him. It helps at this part of the job if the professor can play a harmonica or guitar. It is absolutely essential that he have a keen sense of humor and a quick tongue.

A professor in charge of a field party needs to know first aid; he ought to be able to cook a meal (although he needn't admit it!) and teach cooking to other people. He must see to it that the meals are ample, and are prepared and served on time. He must know the flora, fauna, and geology of the region where he is working. He must be able to make maps, and to teach other people how to make them.

A field archaeologist should know enough about surveying and engineering to lay out and develop his site; enough about photography to be able to keep a pictorial record. If he can

Wood samples can be examined under the microscope

draw as well as photograph, that is an advantage. He needs a mind for detail, so he can organize a field catalog and workshop, and train students to work with them. Whoever officially keeps the field records, the notes are finally the professor's responsibility. Usually he will save each day's notes to go over at night when the other members of the field party have gone to bed. Does this sound easy and absent-minded? It shouldn't.

One last, helpful quality a professor should possess is imagination, but he must know how to control and direct it, so it does not run away with him.

This is a meager outline of what the professor expects to do during part of the year—the two or three months of his summer vacation. In the winter his work is about the same as that of any other university professor. He lectures in classrooms, to student clubs, and to off-campus groups. He finishes, in nine months of directing work in the laboratory and catalog room, the record-keeping that began during the summer's field work. He supervises the cleaning and restoration of archaeological specimens. He grades papers; he travels to and from conferences; once in a while he writes a scientific report or does some original research of his own. He has dinner at home with his family approximately twice a week.

A museum archaeologist, who usually does not have to teach regular classes, *appears* to have an easier life than a university professor does. His work begins where the field work ends as a rule. The museum archaeologist works with the professor at cleaning and restoring specimens, cataloguing them, making and keeping full notes and records about them, and eventually preparing the specimens for display in museum cases. Those same museum cases where we started out to play this archaeology game—remember?

Work of this character requires that the museum archaeologist be deft and skillful in using his hands. Often he is called on to repair or restore fragile, delicate artifacts. He needs some knowledge of chemistry, in order to decide what glues and restorative materials are safest to use with which specimens. I once knew a laboratory archaeologist who took time out to read up on electronics. He perfected a method of cleaning paper-thin, feather-fragile embossed copper breastplates by immersing them in brine and passing a weak electrical current through them. And I know another who spent his outside hours for a year studying the animal life of a certain region. He wanted to identify the beasts engraved on some shell gorgets.

The museum archaeologist gets stoop-shouldered and a backache without even knowing it, from bending over work tables. When he feels he needs a rest and a change of pace, he is likely to take his wife downtown on a window-shopping tour. While she looks at dresses and new hats, he studies the way the merchandise is displayed. In that way he can keep up-to-date on display methods to be used in his museum.

I expect that the archaeologists who most nearly embody what most people mean when they say "archaeologist" are those of the National Park Service. They work out of doors the year round, concentrating directly on the material from the park or monument where they have been assigned. They also, for at least six months of the year, take tourists on guided tours of the ruins, watch out, tactfully, to make sure those same tourists don't pick up and carry away archaeological specimens; answer thousands of questions a week that have nothing on earth to do with archaeology; get up in the middle of a cold mountain night to rescue park visitors who have climbed up cliffs and can't climb down; are responsible for seeing that the wildlife in their territory isn't killed or injured by smart-aleck, out-of-season hunters or well-meant overfeeding, and show little Johnny and Mary the way to the rest rooms, and Johnny's and Mary's parents the way to the picnic grounds. Over and over and over. It takes a strong back and legs, and an even stronger spirit, to become and remain a Park Service archaeologist.

Yet all the time these trained archaeologists, men and women, are doing what they are doing because they love it. They stick to their jobs because the mystery of unanswered questions about other human beings will not let them go. They don't earn much money as compared to garage mechanics, hotel cooks, or good stenographers. But what they have they earn happily, with a feeling of accomplishment and adventure. Few enough people can say so much.

15 The Hobby Archaeologist

THIS IS "YOUR" CHAPTER. IT IS PROBABLY THE ONE THAT YOU have waded through the rest of the book to find. You are earning your living in some other field or are going to school; you haven't the time or inclination to become a full-time twenty-six-hour-a-day archaeologist. At the same time, you are interested in archaeology—in its problems, and also in its theories, as well as its specimens. Is there a place in the world for the hobby archaeologist, or have the professionals got the whole thing "sewed up in a sack and the string bit off"?

Certainly, there is always a place for hobby archaeologists. Most states, and many cities and counties as well, have well-organized, active hobby archaeology groups. These societies are made up of people of all ages, sizes, occupations, and both sexes. Once in a while a group is inactive, but the majority of such local organizations accomplish a lot of good work. They cooperate with professionals in doing excavations. They sponsor or establish community museums. Often their meetings are actually classes in archaeology. These societies invite professionals in to lecture to them, and the members of the associations read reports on work that has been done in other regions.

Some adult archaeology societies sponsor junior groups. In other communities the junior groups are organized as independent research units. The Explorer Scouts and the Senior Girl Scouts have made valuable contributions to scientific archaeology. Whether you belong to one of these advanced groups or not, if you can find other young people who share your interest in archaeology, you can form a junior group in your own community. You had better have at least one older person, who is also interested in archaeology, as a sponsor. There may be times when you will need the backing of an informed and responsible adult.

Otherwise, you can operate on your own. You can draw up a charter and apply for a state excavation license; you can have a constitution, bylaws, and dues, if you wish. Or you can form yourselves into a group that meets informally to visit museums, read reports and papers, and generally kick around archaeological facts and theories. There are a few things, though, that every junior group should do, whether its organization is formal or informal:

1. Learn the provisions of your state's antiquities law, and pledge yourselves to obey it at all times.

2. Find out where the nearest museum with an archaeological collection is located. Learn the name and title of the person in charge of the collection. Meet him, and explain what you would like to do with his help. If you can, find out his field work plans, or you may unknowingly spoil a site he has planned to excavate in his next field season. At all times, be guided by his advice and caution. Work *with* trained archaeologists as much as they will let you. You are both on the same side to begin with, and you will profit immeasurably from the experience. At the same time, don't expect busy people in any field to devote much of their time to you until they are sure that you are worth it. Nobody ever wins by trying to be smarty-pants and show up the experts.

3. Ask if the museum needs volunteer workers to help with repair work and cataloguing, and offer your services—under direction. You can learn a lot by doing. Among other things, you can learn whether you want to go on doing that kind of work or not.

4. Find out if your town or school has a junior museum program, who is in charge of it, and whether you can have display space in the museum for your photographs or specimens.

5. Don't be disappointed if at first other people don't seem to respond to your finds, your books, and your pictures and maps as enthusiastically as you do. They won't. You're doing it, they aren't. If you want them to get steamed up about archaeology, invite them to join you.

6. And most important of all, remember always that you are part of a team, not a star solo player. There are no stars in archaeology. Relationships are more important than things, as we have said again and again, and the only way you can really learn relationships is through teamwork.

It isn't hard to start and set up a local or school museum, if you really want to. The hardest part, usually, is the first thing you have to do: finding a place to put your displays. You may start your museum in a family garage, or in a corner of the parish hall of your church, or in a small display case set in a school corridor. Schools are crowded these days, and finding space for even a small display may turn out to be a headache for your principal. All the same, you'd better start by consulting him. Maybe he *likes* aspirin.

Wherever you eventually do locate your museum display— and even before you start displaying specimens—think seriously about work and storage space. A good rule, one which architects are urged to follow in designing museums, is this: *one* part display space for *four* parts work and storage space. Make sure you have a place to put your specimens and to do needed work on them, before you do anything else.

Don't even start out thinking that you have to have specimens in order to have a display. Some of the greatest museums in the world exhibit nothing but pictures. Some of the most exciting exhibitions ever shown—the Museum of Modern Art's

great storytelling display *The Family of Man,* for example—
have been made up entirely of photographs and labels. Perhaps your state university can lend your group pictures and
labels for such an exhibition. Or perhaps someone in your
home community will have pictures you can use; you can call
on the senior archaeological group sometimes for assistance
in such projects.

Let's talk about displaying specimens only briefly, because
it is a huge subject. True museum display, as was said earlier
in this book, means showing artifacts, as nearly as possible,
as they were originally seen. It means explaining what the
artifacts are, what they are made of, and, if possible, how they
were made. It means telling the use and intention of the artifact. A display that leaves observers guessing about such funda-
mental facts as to whether an object is a knife or a spear point
is a poor display.

For instance, since we have started with them, a collection
of stone points of all sizes, shapes, colors, and stones, glued on
a board in the outline of an Indian head wearing a war bonnet,
is a waste, not a display. It doesn't matter how many points
there are on a square foot of the board. *One* point, mounted
on a neutral background in a small shadow-box frame, with
a label to tell when and where and how it was found, whether
it was on or under the surface, what kind of stone it is and
what type of flaking was used in making it, as well as whether
it has been identified with any group of prehistoric or modern

Indians, is a *display*. This will really tell people something about Indian projectile points or knives when they look at it.

Put your other points away carefully, making sure that each one is identified and identifiable. When your first specimen has been on display for a while, and people have had a chance to look at it and study it if they want to, change your display. Take the first point and its label out of the frame, and put a new specimen and label in their place.

And vary the material you display. Don't use stone points and nothing but stone points, week in and week out. Alternate them with hide scrapers, or with potsherds, or with fragments of matting, or strings of shell or seed beads, depending on where you live and what you have to show. People will be much more likely to keep coming back and looking again if they know they won't see the same tired old point every time.

Vary the backgrounds against which you display your specimens. Don't mount everything you own on monk's cloth or against pale-blue cotton; try red or black or maroon or green or yellow or white—or any other color that you happen to feel like trying. A good idea is to mix small amounts of color with show-card paints, cover cards with them, and put your specimens up against the card for comparison. In that way you can tell whether you have a good or bad color for that particular artifact. Then, if you like, you can go to the trouble and expense of getting a piece of cloth or a painted board as a background. It is just as satisfactory to use a larger painted card, in many cases.

Give your display frame a fresh coat of paint to harmonize with the new backgrounds as you use them. Try typing or writing your labels on colored paper instead of on white or buff, for a change. There are all sorts of display tricks you can use to make your exhibition fresh and interesting. Observe the display methods in use whenever you visit a museum; teach yourself to look at the way exhibitions are put together, as well as at the specimens they contain. Watch department-store windows, and notice how professional display men emphasize one article without obscuring another.

If you have no other way of getting your exhibition before your public, enter it in your school's science fair. Archaeology is a science, and there have been fine and informative archaeological displays included in science fairs in many parts of the United States.

Repair and restoration of museum specimens are specialized parts of display work. Don't think that just because something was broken or torn when it reached you, all you have to do is glue or sew it together for it to look new again. If you can, consult your local museum for the best ways of restoring different kinds of specimens. If you can't, look up the list of textbooks on the subject in the bibliography of this book. The list ought to be longer; there aren't enough such books written. And you and your group can subscribe to *The Mu-*

seum Newsletter, and get information from it, every other month, about the latest repair and display techniques and materials in use in museums all over the United States.

If you want a book from this bibliography and can't find it in your school library, ask the nearest public library in town to get it for you, or, if you live out in the country, write to your State Library Extension Division, and try to get it there. Perhaps you may discover that your local museum has a library, and that you can see the book there. There are all kinds of ways nowadays of getting printed material without buying it.

And, above everything else, remember that you are on the trail of the world's biggest game—Man himself. You are part of a treasure hunt that will go on as long as people live and die, are born and married and buried—as long as cities are built upon cities. You are playing—against time and the weather—a great and exciting game. If you find that you are getting bored with archaeology, stop right where you are. Don't force yourself to go on. Archaeologists have only one universal phrase; their greeting and their parting words are: Have Fun!

State Antiquities Laws

These laws vary widely from state to state. This is a summary of available information, which is intended as a guide to acquiring more. Write to the designated agency in your state to find out what you may and may not do there.

ALABAMA: The archaeological program falls under the State Geological Survey. The law claims and protects all archaeological material within the state as state property.

ARIZONA: The program is integrated with the University of Arizona. The law protects all archaeological material on public land within the state.

ARKANSAS: The program is under the University of Arkansas. There is no state antiquities law.

CALIFORNIA: The archaeology program of the state is operated by and through the University of California, in cooperation with the Division of Beaches and Parks, Department of Natural Resources. The law prohibits vandalism of Indian ruins.

COLORADO: The program is under the University of Colorado. There is no state antiquities law.

CONNECTICUT: The state has no archaeological program, and no antiquities laws.

DELAWARE: The state has an archaeological salvage program. Its antiquities law protects all archaeological material on public land within the state.

FLORIDA: The program is conducted by the University of Florida, the State Museum, and the State Historical Society. There is no antiquities law.

GEORGIA: The program is conducted by the University of Georgia and the State Historical Commission. There is no antiquities law.

IDAHO: The program is conducted by the University of Idaho. There is no antiquities law.

ILLINOIS: The archaeological program is integrated with the University of Illinois and with the State Museum. There is no antiquities law.

INDIANA: The program is directed by the State Historical Society. There is no antiquities law.

IOWA: The archaeological program is directed by the University of Iowa. The law protects all graves from being disturbed.

KANSAS: The program is integrated with the University of Kansas and the State Historical Society. There is no antiquities law.

KENTUCKY: The program is integrated with the University of Kentucky and the Division of Archaeology, Department of Conservation and State Development. There is no antiquities law.

LOUISIANA: The program is jointly operated by the University of Louisiana, the State Museum, and the state commission of Parks and Recreation. There is no antiquities law.

MAINE: No state archaeological program and no antiquities law.

MARYLAND: No state archaeological program and no antiquities law.

MASSACHUSETTS: No state archaeological program and no antiquities law.

MICHIGAN: There are no data available on integration of programs between the State Historical Commission and the universities of the state. The antiquities law protects all archaeological material on public land within the state.

MINNESOTA: The program is integrated with the University of Minnesota. The law claims and protects all archaeological material within the state as state property.

MISSISSIPPI: The state archaeological program is integrated with the University of Mississippi. The antiquities law claims and protects all archaeological material within the state as state property.

MISSOURI: The program is integrated with the University of Missouri. There is no state antiquities law.

MONTANA: The program is integrated with the University of Montana. There is no state antiquities law.

NEBRASKA: The program is coordinated between the University of Nebraska and the State Historical Commission. There is no antiquities law.

NEW HAMPSHIRE: No state archaeological program and no antiquities law.

NEW JERSEY: No data were available on the state program or the antiquities law.

NEW MEXICO: The program is under the joint direction of the University of New Mexico and the New Mexico State Museum. The antiquities law protects all archaeological material on public land within the state.

NEW YORK: The program is integrated with the State Museum. The law protects all archaeological material on public land within the state.

NORTH CAROLINA: The program is operated by and through the University of North Carolina with the cooperation of the State Historical Commission. The law protects all archaeological material on public land within the state.

NORTH DAKOTA: The program is integrated with the State Historical Society. The law claims and protects all archaeological material within the state as state property.

OHIO: The program is conducted by the State Historical Society. There is no antiquities law.

OKLAHOMA: The Oklahoma Archaeological Salvage Program is operated through and by the University of Oklahoma. The law protects all archaeological material on public land within the state.

OREGON: The program is integrated with the University of Oregon. The law protects all archaeological material on public land within the state.

PENNSYLVANIA: The program is coordinated among the University of Pennsylvania, the State Museum, and the State Historical Commission, and is operated by and through the State Museum. There is no antiquities law.

RHODE ISLAND: There is no state archaeological program and no antiquities law.

SOUTH CAROLINA: There is no state archaeological program and no antiquities law.

SOUTH DAKOTA: The State Archaeological Program is operated through and by the University of South Dakota. The antiquities law protects all archaeological material on public land within the state.

TENNESSEE: The program integrates the work of the University of Tennessee and of the State Commission of Parks and Recreation. There is no antiquities law.

TEXAS: The program is integrated with the University of Texas. The law protects all archaeological material on public land within the state.

UTAH: The program is integrated with the University of Utah. The law protects all archaeological material on public land within the state.

VERMONT: There is no state program and no antiquities law.

VIRGINIA: There is no state program and no antiquities law.

WASHINGTON: The program of the State Historical Commission is integrated with that of the University of Washington and is operated by and through the University. The law protects all graves from being disturbed.

WEST VIRGINIA: Temporarily, there is no state archaeological program and no antiquities law. This situation may have been corrected by the time you read this.

WISCONSIN: There is an integrated program carried on by the University of Wisconsin and the State Historical Society. There is no antiquities law.

WYOMING: There is an integrated program carried on by the University of Wyoming and the State Historical Commission. There is no antiquities law.

(This table is based on information compiled by the American Anthropological Association in 1958.)

General Background Information

Anderson, Edgar. *Plants, Man, and Life*. Boston: Little, Brown, 1952.

Bibby, Geoffrey. *Testimony of the Spade*. New York: Knopf, 1956.

Catlin, George. *Letters and Notes on the Manners, Customs, and Condition of the North American Indians . . .* 2 vols. London: Published by the author, 1841.

Ceram, C. W. *Gods, Graves, and Scholars*. New York: Knopf, 1954.

Cole, Sonia. *Counterfeit*. New York: Abelard-Schuman, 1956.

Collier, John. *Indians of the Americas*. New York: Mentor, 1948.

Culin, Stewart. *Games of the North American Indians*. Bureau of American Ethnology, Annual Report No. 24. Washington, D. C.: Government Printing Office, 1902–1903.

Denver Art Museum. *Indian leaflets series*. Denver, Colo.: Published by the Museum, v.d.

Douglas, Frederic H. and d'Harnoncourt, Rene. *Indian Art of the United States*. New York: Museum of Modern Art, 1941.

Field, Henry. *The Track of Man*. Garden City, New York: Doubleday, 1953.

Griffin, James B. *Archaeology of the Eastern United States*. Chicago: University of Chicago Press, 1952.

Hibben, Frank C. *Prehistoric Man in Europe*. Norman, Okla.: University of Oklahoma Press, 1958.

Hodge, Frederic Webb, ed. *Handbook of American Indians North of Mexico*. Bureau of American Ethnology, Bulletin 30. Washington, D. C.: Government Printing Office, 1910.

Hoebel, E. Adamson, Jennings, Jesse D. and Smith, Elmer R. *Readings in Anthropology*. New York: McGraw-Hill, 1955.

Kroeber, A. L. *Cultural and Natural Areas of Native North America*. Berkeley, Calif.: University of California, 1953.

La Farge, Oliver. *Pictorial History of the American Indian*. New York: Crown, 1956.
Mangelsdorf, P. C. and Reeves, R. G. "Origin of Maize." In *American Anthropologist,* n.s. Vol. 47, No. 2. April-June, 1945.
Martin, Paul S., Quimby, George I. and Collier, Donald. *Indians before Columbus*. Chicago, Ill.: University of Chicago Press, 1947.
Mason, Otis Tufton. *Indian Basketry; Studies in a Textile Art without Machinery*. 2 vols. New York: Doubleday, 1904.
Montagu, Ashley. *Man: His First Million Years*. New York: Mentor, 1957.
Place, Robin. *Down to Earth: A Practical Guide to Archaeology*. New York: Philosophical Library, 1955.
Saunderson, Mont H. *Western Land and Water Use*. Norman, Okla.: University of Oklahoma Press, 1950.
Schoolcraft, Henry Rowe. *Historical and Statistical Information Respecting the History, Condition, and Prospects of the Indian Tribes of the United States*. Bureau of American Ethnology, volumes 1–6. Washington, D. C.: Government Printing Office, 1864.
Swanton, John R. *The Indian Tribes of North America*. Bureau of American Ethnology, Bulletin 145. Washington, D. C.: Government Printing Office, 1953.
Underhill, Ruth Murray. *Red Man's America*. Chicago, Ill.: University of Chicago Press, 1953.
Weiner, J. S. *The Piltdown Forgery*. London: Oxford Univ. Press, 1955.
Weltfish, Gene. *Origins of Art*. Indianapolis, Ind.: Bobbs, Merrill, 1953.
Wissler, Clark. *The American Indian*. New York: McMurtrie, 1917.
Wormington, M. H. *Ancient Man in North America*. Denver, Colo.: Denver Museum of Natural History, 1949.
Wright, Muriel H. *Guide to the Indian Tribes of Oklahoma*. Norman, Okla.: University of Oklahoma Press, 1951.

NORTHEASTERN STATES

Bolton, Reginald Pelham. *An Aboriginal Chert Quarry in Northern Vermont*. New York: Museum of the American Indian, Heye Foundation, 1930.
———. *Indian Remains in Northern Vermont*. New York: Museum of the American Indian, Heye Foundation, 1930.
Cross, Dorothy. *Archaeology of New Jersey*. Trenton, New Jersey: Archaeological Society of New Jersey, 1956.
Holmes, W. H. *Aboriginal Pottery of the Eastern United States*. Bureau of American Ethnology, Annual Report 20. Washington, D. C.: Government Printing Office, 1899.

Orchard, William C. *Archaeological Objects from Shorakapkok,* New York: Museum of the American Indian, Heye Foundation, 1926.

Orchard, F. P. *Matinecoc Site on Long Island.* New York: Museum of the American Indian, Heye Foundation, 1928.

Saville, Marshall H. *On Certain Archaeological Specimens from New England.* New York: Museum of the American Indian, Heye Foundation, 1929.

Thomas, Cyrus. *Burial Mounds of the Northern Sections of the United States.* Bureau of American Ethnology, Annual Report 5. Washington, D. C.: Government Printing Office, 1883–1884.

SOUTHEASTERN STATES

Fishwick, Marshall. "Was John Smith a Liar?" *American Heritage,* Vol. IX, No. 6, Oct. 1956.

Flannery, Regina. *Some Notes on a Few Sites in Beaufort County, South Carolina.* Bureau of American Ethnology, Bulletin 133. Washington, D. C.: Government Printing Office, 1943.

Ford, James A. and Willey, Gordon. "Interpretation of the Prehistory of the Eastern United States." In *American Anthropologist,* n. s. Vol. 43, No. 3, pt. 1. 1941.

Fundburk, Emma Lila. *Southeastern Indians.* Luverne, Ala.: Published by the Author, 1958.

────── and Foreman, Mary Douglass Fundburk: *Sun Circles and Human Hands.* Luverne, Ala.: Published by the Authors, 1957.

Funkhouser, W. D. and Webb, William S. *Rock Shelters of Wolfe and Powell Counties, Kentucky.* Reports in Archaeology and Anthropology, No. 5. Lexington, Ky.: University of Kentucky, 1930.

Griffin, James B. *Analysis and Interpretation of the Ceramic Remains from Two Sites near Beaufort, South Carolina.* Bureau of American Ethnology, Bulletin 133. Washington, D. C.: Government Printing Office, 1943.

Harrington, M. R. *Certain Caddo Sites in Arkansas.* New York: Museum of the American Indian, Heye Foundation, 1920.

──────. *Cherokee and Earlier Remains on Upper Tennessee River.* New York: Museum of the American Indian, Heye Foundation, 1922.

──────. *A New Archaeological Field in Texas.* New York: Museum of the American Indian, Heye Foundation, 1928.

Holmes, William H. *Catalog of Collections Made during the Field Season of 1881.* Bureau of American Ethnology, Annual Report 3. Washington, D. C.: Government Printing Office, 1881.

──────. *Origin and Development of Form and Ornament in Ceramic*

Art. Bureau of American Ethnology, Annual Report 4. Washington, D. C.: Government Printing Office, 1882.

————. *Prehistoric Textile Fabrics of the United States.* Bureau of American Ethnology, Annual Report 3. Washington, D. C.: Government Printing Office, 1881.

————. *Study of the Textile Art.* Bureau of American Ethnology, Annual Report 6. Washington, D. C.: Government Printing Office, 1884.

Lewis, Thomas N. M. and Kneberg, Madeline. *Tribes that Slumber.* Knoxville, Tenn.: University of Tennessee, 1958.

Mook, Maurice A. "Aboriginal Population in Tidewater Virginia." *American Anthropologist,* n.s. Vol. 46, No. 2, pt. 1. April-June, 1944.

Myer, William Edward. *Two Prehistoric Villages in Middle Tennessee.* Bureau of American Ethnology, Annual Report 41. Washington, D. C.: Government Printing Office, 1924.

Royce, Charles C. *The Cherokee Nation of Indians.* Bureau of American Ethnology, Annual Report 5. Washington, D. C.: Government Printing Office, 1883.

Swanton, John R. *Indians of the Southeastern United States.* Bureau of American Ethnology, Bulletin 137. Washington, D. C.: Government Printing Office, 1946.

————. "Notes on the Cultural Province of the Southeast." In *American Anthropologist,* n. s. Vol. 37, No. 3, pt. 1. July-September, 1935.

Thoburn, Joseph B. *Tropical and sub-tropical Origin of Mound-Builder Cultures.* In Chronicles of Oklahoma, Vol. XVI, No. 1, Sec. 1. Oklahoma City, Okla.: Oklahoma Historical Society, 1938.

Turbyfill, Charles O. *Steatite Effigy Pipe from the Old Cherokee Country in North Carolina.* New York: Museum of the American Indian, Heye Foundation, 1928.

Webb, W. S. *Archaeological Survey of Wheeler Basin . . .* Bureau of American Ethnology, Bulletin 122. Washington, D. C.: Government Printing Office, 1939.

————. *Read Shell Midden . . .* Reports in Archaeology and Anthropology, Vol. VII, No. 5. Lexington, Ky.: University of Kentucky, 1950.

———— and De Jarnette, D. L. *Archaeological Survey of Pickwick Basin . . .* Bureau of American Ethnology, Bulletin 129. Washington, D. C.: Government Printing Office, 1942.

———— and Funkhauser, W. D. *Archaeological Survey of Kentucky.* Reports in Archaeology and Anthropology, Vol. II. Lexington, Ky.: University of Kentucky, 1932.

————. *McLeon Bluff Site in Hickman County, Kentucky.* Reports in Archaeology and Anthropology, Vol. III, No. 1. Lexington, Ky.: University of Kentucky, 1933.

————. *Rock Shelters in Menifee County, Kentucky.* Reports in Archaeology and Anthropology, Vol. III, No. 4. Lexington, Ky.: University of Kentucky, 1936.

MISSISSIPPI VALLEY

Chapman, Carl H. "Missouri's Archaeological Site Survey." *Missouri Historical Review.* Vol. XLIX, No. 2. Columbia, Mo.: Missouri Historical Review, 1955.

Dall, W. H. *On Masks, Labrets, and Certain Aboriginal Customs.* Bureau of American Ethnology, Annual Report 3. Washington, D. C.: Government Printing Office, 1881.

Deuel, Thorn. "Basic Cultures of the Mississippi Valley." *American Anthropologist,* n.s. Vol. 37, No. 3, pt. 1. July-September, 1935.

Fowke, Gerard. *Surface Deposits along the Mississippi between the Missouri and Ohio Rivers.* Missouri Historical Society Collections, Vol. III, No. 1. St. Louis, Mo.: Missouri Historical Society, 1908.

Hawley, Florence. *Tree-ring Analysis and Dating in the Mississippi Drainage.* University of Chicago Occasional Papers, No. 2. Chicago, Ill.: University of Chicago, 1941.

Hilder, F. F. *Notes on the Archaeology of Missouri.* Missouri Historical Society Publication, No. 6. St. Louis, Mo.: Missouri Historical Society, n.d.

Holmes, William H. *Ancient Pottery of the Mississippi Valley.* Bureau of American Ethnology, Annual Report 4. Washington, D. C.: Government Printing Office, 1882.

Krieger, Alex D. *Importance of the "Gilmore Corridor" in Culture Contacts between Middle America and Eastern United States.* Bulletin of the Texas Archaeological and Paleontological Society, Vol. 19. Austin, Texas: The Society, 1948.

McDermott, John Francis, ed. *Tixier's Travels on the Osage Prairies.* Norman, Okla.: University of Oklahoma Press, 1940.

Marriott, Alice. "The Cross Timbers as a Cultural Barrier." *Texas Geological Magazine,* Vol. XII, No. 1. Dallas, Texas: The Southwest Review, 1943.

Webb, W. S. and Snow, Charles E. *The Adena People.* Reports in Anthropology, Vol. VI. Lexington, Ky.: University of Kentucky, 1945.

HIGH PLAINS AREA

Clark, W. P. *Indian Sign Language.* Philadelphia, Pa.: 1885.

Coffin, Edwin F. *Archaeological Exploration of a Rock Shelter in Brewster County, Texas.* New York: Museum of the American Indian, Heye Foundation, 1932.

Ewers, John C. "The Case for Blackfoot Pottery." *American Anthropologist,* n. s. Vol. 47, No. 2. April-June, 1945.

Haines, Francis Wister. "Northward Spread of Horses among the Plains Indians." *American Anthropologist,* n. s. Vol. 40, No. 3. July-September, 1938.

Hyde, George E. *Indians of the High Plains.* Norman, Okla.: University of Oklahoma Press, 1959.

Jenks, Albert Ernest. *Minnesota's Brown's Valley Man.* Memoirs of the American Anthropological Association, No. 49, 1937.

Marriott, Alice. *Indians on Horseback.* New York: Crowell, 1948.

Mead, Margaret. *Anthropologist at Work: The Writings of Ruth Benedict.* Boston: Houghton, 1959.

Oetteking, Bruno. *Skeletal Remains from Texas.* New York: Museum of the American Indian, Heye Foundation, 1930.

Roe, Frank Gilbert. *The Indian and the Horse.* Norman, Okla.: University of Oklahoma Press, 1955.

Watson, Virginia. *The Optima Focus of the Panhandle Aspect.* Bulletin of the Texas Archaeological and Paleontological Society, Vol. 21. Lubbock, Texas: 1950.

ANASAZI, HOHOKAM, MIMBRENOS, AND OTHER SOUTHWESTERNERS

Baldwin, Gordon C. "Analysis of Basket Maker III Sandals from Northeastern Arizona." *American Anthropologist,* n. s. Vol. 40, No. 3. July-September, 1938.

Bandelier, Adolf F. *The Delight Makers.* New York: Dodd, 1947.

Cushing, Frank H. *A Study of Pueblo Pottery.* Bureau of American Ethnology, Annual Report 4. Washington, D. C.: Government Printing Office, 1882.

Dickey, Roland. "The Potters of the Mimbres Valley." *New Mexico Quarterly,* Vol. XXVII, Nos. 1, 2. Albuquerque, New Mex.: University of New Mexico, 1957.

Fewkes, Jesse Walter. *Antiquities of the Upper Verde River.* Bureau of American Ethnology, Annual Report 28. Washington, D. C.: Government Printing Office, 1906.

———. *Casa Grande, Arizona.* Bureau of American Ethnology, Annual Report 29. Washington, D. C.: Government Printing Office, 1906.

———. *Hopi Kachinas.* Bureau of American Ethnology, Annual Report 21. Washington, D. C.: Government Printing Office, 1899.

———. *Notes on Tusayan Snake and Flue Ceremonies.* Bureau of American Ethnology, Annual Report 19. Washington, D. C.: Government Printing Office, 1897.

————. *Tusayan Migration Traditions*. Bureau of American Ethnology, Annual Report 19. Washington, D. C.: Government Printing Office, 1897.

————. *Two Summers' Work in Pueblo Ruins*. Bureau of American Ethnology, Annual Report 22. Washington, D. C.: Government Printing Office, 1899.

Gladwin, Harold Sterling. *History of the Ancient Southwest*. Portland, Maine: Bond, Wheelwright Co. 1957.

Goddard, Pliny Earle. *Indians of the Southwest*. New York: American Museum of Natural History, 1931.

Hall, E. T., Jr. "Recent Clues to Athapascan Prehistory in the Southwest." *American Anthropologist*, n. s. Vol. 46, No. 1, pt. 1. January-March, 1944.

Harrington, M. R. *Another Ancient Salt Mine in Nevada*. New York: Museum of the American Indian, Heye Foundation, 1926.

————. *A Pre-Pueblo Site on the Colorado River*. New York: Museum of the American Indian, Heye Foundation, 1926.

————. *Tracing the Pueblo Boundary in Nevada*. New York: Museum of the American Indian, Heye Foundation, 1928.

Hewett, Edgar L. *Ancient Life in the American Southwest*. New York: Tudor, 1943.

Holmes, William H. *Pottery of the Ancient Pueblos*. Bureau of American Ethnology, Annual Report 4. Washington, D. C.: Government Printing Office, 1882.

Ingersoll, Ernest. *Ruins in Southwestern Colorado*. New York: Museum of the American Indian, Heye Foundation, 1928.

McGregor, John C. *Southwestern Archaeology*. New York: Wiley, 1941.

McNichols, Charles L. *Crazy Weather*. New York: Macmillan, 1944.

McNickle, D'Arcy. *Runner in the Sun*. Philadelphia: Winston, 1954.

Marriott, Alice. *Indians of the Four Corners*. New York: Crowell, 1952.

————. *Maria, the Potter of San Ildefonso*. Norman, Okla.: University of Oklahoma Press, 1947.

Mera, Harry P. *Style Trends of Pueblo Pottery*. Santa Fe, New Mex.: Laboratory of Anthropology, 1939.

Mindeleff, Cosmos. *Localization of Tusayan Clans*. Bureau of American Ethnology, Annual Report 19. Washington, D. C.: Government Printing Office, 1897.

Parsons, Elsie Clews. *Pueblo Indian Religion*. 2 vols. Chicago, Ill.: University of Chicago Press, 1939.

Steen, Charlie R. "Slit Tapestry from the Upper Salt River Valley, Arizona." *American Anthropologist*, n. s. Vol. 37, No. 3, pt. 1. July-September, 1935.

Stubbs, Stanley A. *Bird's-eye View of the Pueblos.* Norman, Okla.: University of Oklahoma Press, 1950.

Underhill, Ruth M. *First Penthouse Dwellers of America.* New York: Augustine, n.d.

Waterman, T. T. *Ornamental Designs in Southwestern Pottery.* New York: Museum of the American Indian, Heye Foundation, 1930.

Waters, Frank. *Masked Gods.* Albuquerque, New Mex.: University of New Mexico Press, 1951.

Wilson, Edmund. *Red, Black, Blond, and Olive.* New York: Oxford University Press, 1956.

Wormington, H. M. *Prehistoric Indians of the Southwest.* Denver, Colo.: Denver Museum of Natural History, 1947.

————. *Reappraisal of the Fremont Culture.* Denver, Colo.: Denver Museum of Natural History, 1955.

———— and Lister, Robert H. *Archaeological Investigations on the Uncomphagre Plateau.* Denver, Colo.: Denver Museum of Natural History, 1956.

WEST AND NORTHWEST

Drucker, Philip. *Archaeological Survey on the Northwest Coast.* Bureau of American Ethnology, Bulletin 133. Washington, D. C.: Government Printing Office, 1943.

Goddard, Pliny Earle. *Indians of the Northwest Coast.* New York: American Museum of Natural History, 1934.

Mallery, Garrick. *Pictographs of the North American Indians.* Bureau of American Ethnology, Annual Report 4. Washington, D. C.: Government Printing Office, 1882.

————. *Picture-writing of the American Indians.* Bureau of American Ethnology, Annual Report 10. Washington, D. C.: Government Printing Office, 1888.

Sims, Agnes. *San Cristobal Pictographs.* Santa Fe, New Mex.: Pictograph Press, 1947.

Strong, William Duncan. "Occurrence and Wider Implication of a 'Ghost Cult' on the Columbia River." *American Anthropologist,* n. s. Vol. 47, No. 2, April-June, 1945.

Underhill, Ruth M. *Indians of the Pacific Northwest.* Education Division of the United States Office of Indian Affairs. Riverside, Calif.: Sherman Indian Institute Press, 1944.

AZTECS, MAYAS, AND THE WORLD

Boas, Franz. *Primitive Art*. New York: Dover, 1955.

Caso, Alfonso. *The Aztecs: People of the Sun*. Norman, Okla.: University of Oklahoma Press, 1958.

Fewkes, Jesse Walter. *A Prehistoric Island Culture of America*. Bureau of American Ethnology, Annual Report 34. Washington, D. C.: Government Printing Office, 1913.

Holmes, William H. *Ancient Art of the Province of Chiriqui*. Bureau of American Ethnology, Annual Report 6. Washington, D. C.: Government Printing Office, 1884.

Roth, Walter E. *Inquiry into the Animism and Folk-lore of the Guiana Indians*. Bureau of American Ethnology, Annual Report 30. Washington, D. C.: Government Printing Office, 1909.

Spinden, Herbert J. *Ancient Civilizations of Mexico and Central America*. New York: American Museum of Natural History, 1928.

Tilden, Freeman. *The National Parks: What They Mean to You and Me*. New York: Knopf, 1955.

Vaillant, George C. *The Aztecs of Mexico*. Bungay, Suffolk: Penguin Books, 1956.

———. "Correlation of Archaeological and Historical Sequences in the Valley of Mexico." *American Anthropologist*, n. s. Vol. 40, No. 4, pt. 1, October-December, 1938.

Whiting, Alfred F. "Origin of Corn." *American Anthropologist*, n.s. Vol. 46, No. 4. October-December, 1944.

Index